Yesterday, Today and Forever…My Walk with the Lord

Poetry of Inspiration and Love

Written by

Brenda J. Martin-Linton

ISBN: 1-4107-7899-1 (e-book)
ISBN: 1-4107-7900-9 (Paperback)

This book is printed on acid free paper.

1stBooks - rev. 12/18/03

<u>Preface</u>

TO WHOM IT MAY CONCERN:

I, Ms. Brenda J. Martin-Linton, will take this opportunity to introduce myself. It is through this introduction that I pray you will obtain some insight into the growth and development of my spiritual relationship will God through my poetry.

First of all, during my Christian growth through the years, I have purposed in my heart a closeness with God and love for my fellow man. This relationship can be recognized in my writings. It is through my inspirational poems, love poems and dedications that I share them with others for encouragement in their times of doubt, longing, need and hurt.

Besides writing poetry, I share my love for people through my profession as an elementary school educator. I have a great love for singing Gospel music. I am also the proud mother of two daughters. Sadly though, as of February 23, 1994, I became a widow.

In conclusion, I have learned and written a great deal about God, my fellow man. Yet, I am still growing. Prayerfully, after reading these poems, you may have a better understanding about *__My Walk with the Lord__.* Even more, this book of poetry will be a blessing to you spiritually and enlighten your walk with God.

May God Richly Bless You,

Mrs. Brenda J. Martin-Linton

Introduction

***Yesterday—Today—And Forever: My Walk
With The Lord***
Greetings…my Christian sisters & brothers.
My name, Brenda, & my occupation, an
Educator, is really of little importance or value,
other than for this book—*for I'm just a servant
of the Lord.* I'm just sharing some
inspirational poems with you. I pray that thru
these 'poetic expressions' you'll experience
some comfort…some joy…some assurance—
that God loves you. He cares & loves us so
much that He sent His Son, Jesus, to be
crucified, rise, and ascend back to Him. Jesus
is returning for us (you…you…and even you).
I desire to share ***My Walk With The Lord*** with
you…and perhaps you'll find that we've
journeyed down similar roads during
trials/tribulations. That alone brings us
together…as sisters & brothers in The Lord.
**However, the true comfort in having these
experiences is that you can rest in the fact of
knowing that we've never been alone.** For
Jesus, has been and will always be there with
us; even when we get too tired…weary…or

v

discouraged to continue on. He is the One who carries all of us through these times.

Why the Lord has chosen me to write—I could not tell you. All I know is that thru these 30+ years, He has placed it on my heart to express His presence and dealings with me through poetry. I've just kept them together, never realizing that they were of any value to anyone but myself: for they are expressions of my Love for the Lord; they reflect different periods of my life traveling with the Lord. These poems express my sorrows, my joys, my heartaches, my pain—my times of discouragement—my shortcomings—God's times of disciplining me and my search for The Lord. Yes, to me they only displayed the many time-lines in my life. However, in these last five years, the Lord has encouraged me to put them together. I had no idea why, until that year, *after the death of my husband.* The Lord placed it on my heart to share these times and experiences with others—so that someone may realize the joy of trusting the Lord: even through their hard times.

So here I am, typing, expressing and obeying my Lord…sharing with you…my relatives in the Lord. I need you to help me to get God's

Word & His Love…out to others. We must take our rightful places in our homes…in the community…in the world…proclaiming God's Love. We have to say "no" to worldly things & "yes" to the ways of God. Let's begin to re-establish our morals and values that we once held fast to. In doing these things…we'll give our Lord and Savior all the glory, praise and honor that He so rightly deserves. For God has not only walked with me…but He has also walked with you!!! He was with you my friend…Yesterday…He's with you Today…well, He'll forever be with you. Through our trials & tribulations, *God* fills all voids…He heals all wounds. Remember—in the death of a loved one…there is no loss; for we know if they are in Christ they're with God. *No one is considered as a "loss" when we know where they are!!!*

In this "inspirational book of poetry", I desire to share my "poetic" life experiences with you. It gives me great pleasure, to be selected by God to perform such a task. I have asked for God's guidance in this, as I've tried to do in the 'totality' of my life. Believe me…I am in no way special or perfect: for I was a sinner.

But by grace, Jesus saved me. I'm just *one* of God's children who chose Jesus. As readers of ***The Past...Present...and Forever: My Walk With The Lord Ministry,*** I'm praying for these 3 things from you. 1) Please allow me to share in you hurts & your joys in the ministry of my poetic life experiences. 2) Share these words of spiritual expressions with others. 3) Let our walk in the Lord always bring all the Glory, Honor & Praise to Him. I will now share a poem the Lord blessed me to write when my husband died. It has brought great comfort to my soul.

<u>Jesus—Help Me Make It...Thru These Lonely Nights</u>

At this very moment—loneliness fills my
heart…
For I feel all alone—Please Jesus don't You
from me part;

I need Your loving arms to hold me very tight;
Please Dear Jesus help me make it thru these
lonely nights.

Since Leonard's death, I tossed & turned
greatly thru the night;
When I fell asleep, nightmares kept me in
much fright;

Again Lord, I'm alone, I need something from
You…
Now my husband has gone home, God—I need
You!

This loneliness Lord, really hurts—it tears at
my very soul…
For I had companionship…now I am alone;

I need You to be with me…and to love me too…
Although Leonard has gone Home—I know I will need You!

God don't let me cry myself- to sleep again tonight…
Draw me in Your loving arms/ cuddle me very tight;

Lord don't turn your back on me—Yes, to me stay true…
For there is no comfort if…I'm not loved by You!!!

So, please, Lord—understand—Love is a great need…
For to love and be loved back is one way to be free;

Free from the loneliness—that escalates at night…
Please, Jesus help me make it thru these many lonely nights!!!

Written by God's Child and Servant,
Brenda J. Linton

Dedications and Acknowledgements

Dedicated to Jesus, who is my Lord and
Savior,
my husband, Marion [Leonard] Linton, my
mother, Ella Mae Bonds and my two
daughters,
April and Isis.

I wish to thank my two daughters April and
Isis for the proof reading of my book. I also
give thanks to my sister Tall Rosa and all
the people who encouraged me to complete
my book for publishing. I thank Isis for the
poem she wrote. I used it in the closing of
my book.
Thanks be to God for everyone whom He
has put into my life to help me to walk this
walk of
Faith.

Thank God for all of you.

Table of Contents

Dedications

Inspirational
Poetry

Brenda J. Martin-Linton

<u>Tomorrow Is Not Promised</u>

Tomorrow is not promised to you,
Please don't deceive yourself;
So give God your life, your heart, your
soul,
He's your only source of help.

Tomorrow is not promised to you,
So get on with God's work;
Stop dragging your feet and
procrastinating,
Your duties you shouldn't shirk.

Tomorrow is not promised to you,
So realize that fact right now;
For today you live—today you die.
So there's an urgency to serve Him.

So repeat in your heart this message
now,
Tomorrow is not promised to you;
The sooner you realize this in your heart,
God's work you will readily do.

3

<u>Forgiveness</u>

Lord, I thank You for forgiving me...
For dying on the cross;
You hung, bled, and died for me—
So my soul would not be lost.

But Your death wasn't just for me...
It was for this world so full of sin;
That our Heavenly Father sent You for—
To give us life again.

To give us life again from death...
Because of our sinful nature;
Lord, thank You again, I say—
For You are the only One who could
save us.

Your dying kept me from going be hell.
Spending an eternity in hell fire;
.I cry when I think of how You
suffered—But Your Courage—
I love and admire.

4

So Lord, I come…with this request…
As I think about everyday life;
Please help me…to forgive my
neighbor—
In this day of sorrow and strife!!!

<u>Thanks Be to God</u>

To give thanks to someone,
Who's been very kind to you;
Should never be a chore…
For anyone to do!

To give thanks is a way…
To show one's appreciation;
And that much I can do for God—
Without the slightest hesitation!

In fact, it gives me such great joy…
To give thanks to my Lord and God;
For He is responsible for my existence…
And He's with me where e'er I may trod.

He's with me each and every night
Even when I'm fast asleep;
He's with me during the busy day—
It's my interest at heart He keeps.

So come on…It shouldn't be that hard
To give thanks to my Lord, Jesus Christ;
***Because really—without God's
existence…***
We'd have no hope for…Eternal Life!!!

Brenda- I'm As Close As Your Phone

Jesus you are so wonderful,
In every single way;
You have kept your many promises,
Each and every day!

Why can't I remember this?
When trouble comes in my direction?
I must learn, Lord, to depend on,
Your promises and continuous affection!

You've come through each and every
time,
You've never left me alone;
I must remember…yes…remember- oh,
You are as close as my telephone.

So the next time I go through a dilemma,
And try to solve it alone;
Please *whisper*—SCREAM—SHOUT
OR YELL...
**"BRENDA, I'M AS CLOSE AS
YOUR TELEPHONE!!!!!!!!!!!!!!"**

<u>I'm Still Searching...Since 1971</u>
<u>And Before</u>

Dear God:

For many years now I've been searching,
Looking everywhere for You;
I've done everything and been
everywhere,
Please tell me what more can I do?

I've attended many churches, my Lord,
I've talked to ones who have confessed;
I've read materials on all those blessed,
Please tell me so I can rest.

Rest from searching in the wrong places,
Rest from hearing others confess...
Cause I want to know for myself,
Yes, I would like to be blessed.

So please don't be a puzzle-
With the pieces are all scattered apart—
I want to know You for myself,
God, I want You in my heart!

Brenda J. Martin-Linton

<u>(God's Conversation With Me)</u>
<u>God's Forgiveness or Forgive Me</u>
<u>God</u>

Why should I forgive you?
You know what you did was wrong!
You know you had a different
destination,
Before you left from home!

But you—just—followed them.
Brenda, Please tell me—Why?
Tell me the honest…The whole truth—
And don't tell me a lie!!!

You gave me…your very oath—
That you would do much better…
And that—day by—day by day
You would write me a letter.

But yesterday...you forgot-
I guess you had something more
important to do...
Now tell me—my servant, Brenda,
What if I forgot you!

Brenda what's...wrong with you?
I thought you were going to rebuke
wrong;
And daily sing praises to Me,
Lifting up your voice in song!

But I'll try to un-der-stand—
'Cause for your sins I did die;
I'll forgive you because I gave My
Word...
Forgive you in spite of the lie...(After
all you did try.)

Brenda J. Martin-Linton

I'm Getting Closer to Knowing Who You Are (1987)

**Lord, I think I'm getting closer—
To knowing who "You" are;**
I'm beginning to really realize…
That you haven't been that far!

You haven't been as far as I thought—
In all my years of searching for You;
Looking around I can see from Your
Works…
That there are millions and millions of
clues!!!

Clues to let me know of Your Marvelous
Beauty—
From the green grass to the beautiful sky;
From the birds in the air to the leaves on
the trees,
I can see You through my own eyes!

I can see You as the wind blows through
the trees—
I can see You when the clouds shed their
tears;
I can't believe that I didn't see You,
In all of my searching years.

***It's so beautiful to finally know that I'm
closer—***
To know just who and what You are;
It's not You who's been away from
me—
It's me who's been away from You...SO
FAR.

<u>Death</u>

Some folks are scared to die,
I am too—that is no lie
After death—I am hoping I might,
If it's "Thy Will"—to sit on your right.

Yet, I would still like to know…
What is death like, and where does one go?
This is one answer the dead can't bring back;
And also one answer the living man's
knowledge lack!!!

****

<u>Dear God,</u>

Instill in me—the Love of Thee,
That is in Your Word;
Help me to think of You as,
The only One to serve!!!

****

<u>Life</u>

The Lord giveth life,
The Lord taketh it away—
Lord please be good to me,
On that Great Judgment Day.

"Who Am I? God"

I am *lonely, sad, worn and confused*—
I am **ostracized, rebuked, mocked and used;**
I am lost as a sheep from the fold,
I am alone, I don't even have a hope.

I am happy at times, then I tend to shout—
While at other times, I have reason to doubt;
I am with a friend having fun in song—
I am by myself—"Why am I always alone?"

Oh, God, I love sometimes, then I am glad—
Yet I dislike sometimes…This makes me sad;
Tell me," Why am I so Lonely and blue?"
I guess I am alone God…When I forget You!!!

****

Poetry .
Of Love

Brenda J. Martin-Linton

Love Is; Life Can…

Love is giving; *Love is* sharing—
Love is doing; *Love is caring*

Love is beautiful; *Love is* few—
Love is everything; *Love is (God)*, You.

Life can be exciting; *Life can* be so new—
Life can be so beautiful…***Just being with You!!!***

****

Who? What? Why?

Who is my keeper?
Who is my friend?
Who cares for me…
When the day ends?

What is His purpose?
What does He do?
Why does He have to keep me still?
When I want to move?

Why am I being watched?
Why is His Eye on me?
Why is it that I am blind—
When He wants me to see?

The Lord is my "Keeper,"
He is with me always;
He watches over me,
Regardless of the time of day!

"Where Are You, (God) Dear?"

Oh, I have looked far—and have looked
near,
I have looked there—and I have looked
here—
Tell me……
Where are you God dear?

I have told my friends to be on the
lookout;
If they hear anything just give a loud
shout!!!
But to no avail, I thought that would
do…
Tell me my **"Dear God, where are
you?"**

But I'll just keep on looking without a
pause,
Trying my best to locate You because…
I can't sleep nor slumber—or rest
without You,
Or think of others who in numbers are
few.

I can't take no rest or little break,
Until every avenue I overtake;
Because to me without You anywhere
near…
The question keeps coming, **"Where are
You, God, Dear?"**

<u>I Love…</u>
<u>I Am Loved…</u>
<u>I Long To Love!!!!!</u>

Lord You know without a doubt,
That I love You with all my heart;
My love for You is so genuine,
I pray that we never part.

For Our Love is Everlasting…
At least I know Yours is;
But I want You to know that I want to
give,
You all the love a human can give—(as
long as I live).

No one on earth can destroy this love,
That I possess for only You!
For You're the Number
One…"Uno"…The First…
This love I give only to You!!!

But Lord I want to ask this of You,
It is wrong for me to request:
A friend—a husband—someone to care,
Someone whom You think is best?

Best for me to share my life,
And for him to share his life with me;
Lord, I long to love someone…
If it'd be alright with Thee!

So yes, I love You…Dearly…Lord,
And yet I long for someone to love;
Though I know within my heart,
True Love comes from—YOU—above.

<u>Material Things</u>

From the very first beginning
Man chose to serve other things
Besides serving the true and Living God,
He built images to worship
He maintained his wealth
He bought wardrobes of items
But he neglected one thing
His spiritual health!

Yes, man performed these practiced,
He worshipped Baal and burned candles
He prayed to the devil and dwelt in
séances
He played the horses and numbers
hoping much
He even ventured in tents hoping in
gypsies
To foretell his luck!

But why has man done these things?
Putting his heart in material things…
Because there is so much in life
And there is so much in life
That spiritual health instead of material
Will become our footsteps when we trod!

<u>Everywhere I Go</u>

Jesus, You go everywhere with me.
I would like to say…
I do not know where I'd be,
Without You throughout the day.

You are with me when I'm awake,
When I first open my eyes;
I pray and thank you everywhere,
For staying by my side!

You're with me even when I go out,
You're right there by my side;
You never ever take a break from me,
Not even for a joy ride.

As I prepare my busy schedule,
To follow throughout the day…
I know that I need not be afraid,
'Cause You're with me to stay.

I feel Your presence while driving to work.
I sing praises to Your Name;
When others look and see me singing,
I never feel ashamed.

I feel You daily on my job;
I feel You when I'm alone;
I feel You when I'm praying,
I feel You when I return home.

Yes Lord, You are everywhere I go,
From daybreak until dawn;
I am blessed to have You always with me,
For with You I am never alone!!!

<u>God's Creation</u>

Look around you—tell me, "What do
you see?"
The sky, the sun, the grass, the trees;
People…Animals…Alive and dead,
Insects all over—No matter where one
treads!

****

<u>(Dear God) Help Me!!!!!</u>

Help me to journey through the world
below,
Help me to love my neighbor—to let my
love to show,
Help me to my fellow man to try to
understand,
Help me to lend everyone—A helping
hand.

Help me to believe—To believe only in
You,
Help me to keep the faith—And to You
be true;
Help me to see the light—That You
would have me see,
Help me to be whatever—Lord…You
desire me to be.

(Cure For) Loneliness: Look in the Bible

When you are there with no one to share,
All of those long and wondering
thoughts;
Then it comes a time for you to look for
that lost dream,
The one which you once had thought!

You had looked here and there…In fact
you had looked everywhere;
Until you had given up all hope and
desire,
And then one day when you looked in
your Bible,
You saw something which was once
admired.

33

Brenda J. Martin-Linton

Give Your Mind To Jesus (Song)

Give your mind to Jesus, my Lord
Only He can see you through;
Just trust in Him and His Holy Word,
He can make your life A-new.

Give your mind to Jesus, my God,
Your path He can direct;
He's God's only Son-and He's the Only
One,
Whom we can serve…While He
protects.

He means more to me than life itself,
Without Jesus I would surely fail;
My mind belongs to Jesus my Lord,
Just like a ship has a sail.

I Do Love You Lord God,

I really do love You Lord…with all my
heart and soul,
I need to ask some things of
You…Please Lord make me Whole;
I need You in my life. In everything I do
'Cause I can't breathe…talk…Or do
anything without You.

I realize that only You Lord…Hold
everything in Your precious Hands,
By this I mean without You Lord…I
can't even stand;
I don't even have the smallest
chance…Without You by my side.
That's why I need You in my heart…To
live and to abide!

Sometimes I guess I do forget…To
confide and come to You,
And then I end up feeling like…A
number one "Class A" fool;

So Lord I ask that during these times
You will always protect me,
Because if **You search me, really
search me...** You'll know...
I Do Love Thee!!!

Please Don't Fish in the Water:
No Fishing Allowed (Song)

1. Why do you always bring up the past,
Whenever we meet and talk;
Why must all my old mistake last,
In your memories each day you walk.

2. Every time I go to visit,
So called friends in their home;
They dwell on the past-it just lasts and
lasts,
They won't leave my past alone.

3. Sometimes I sit and wonder,
What does in my future lie;
For whenever I go-everyone lets me
know,
That my past will never die.

Brenda J. Martin-Linton

<u>Chorus</u>

**Please don't fish in the water
For things I'd rather forget,
For God sunk them there in the water;
He never brings them up for air,
For there is no fishing allowed.**

<u>Jesus Knew…Did You? His Choice</u>

<u>Vs. #1</u>
Did you know why Jesus Christ was born?
Did you know why the angels blew their horns?
Did You Know Why my Savior had to die
let me Tell you, Child, the reasons "Why".

My Lord Jesus knew before Creation
About the year of His Crucifixion
He knew He'd disrobe Himself and come down to earth
He Knew His mother, his purpose and his birth.

My Lord, Jesus, knew that men would live in sin
So, Sweet Jesus chose to live among men
Jesus knew about his life that man would take
Jesus knew The sacrifice that he would make.

39

****
****

<u>Vs. #2</u>

Did you know why the angels sounded
their horn?
They knew the year that Jesus would be
born.
So they prepared their horns from the very
start
They put the heavenly music in our sinful
hearts.

Did you know why my sweet Savior chose
to die?
He looked from Heaven and Tears rolled
down from His (Tender) eyes
He could not bear the fact of Hell as man's
destiny
So He disrobed Himself and chose to die
for you and me.

****
****

Refrain v.1&2

Did you know about My Lord before
Creation?
Did you know the year of my Saviors
crucifixion?
Did you know That Jesus would disrobe
and come to Earth?
Did you know about His mother and His
Birth?

Vs. #3

Jesus knew about his birth, life and death
He knew abut heaven and eternal health
He knew that on earth man would surely
die
So My Savior chose to die for you and I.

So let us live and give Jesus Christ the
praise
Knowing that one day our spirits He will
raise
We should honor his death and live a
Christian Life
By thanking Him morning, noon and night.

Refrain v.3

So, yes, My Jesus Christ, my lord and
savior knew
He knew from the beginning Oh Let me
ask "did you?"
Thank God He did know and he did what
had to be done
He Chose to die for us...God's only Son.

<u>True Love</u>

There are many kinds of love,
That one may possess;
But no matter how you may love,
It's love nevertheless.

Though some people love for money,
And some people love for riches;
This is the kind of love,
That can be buried in ditches.

Some people love spiritually,
Because God told them to;
This is the greatest of all the "loves",
And this love is "Oh" so true.

****

<u>You Are My Doctor</u>

Lord, I feel quite weak at this time,
But, I still want to drop You a line;
Please, Lord, hear me as I speak,
Because I beg You to keep;
Me in Your arms and in Your care,
For You are my only Doctor.

<u>You Are My Friend</u>

Lord I love you so very, very much…
That I can't live without your tender
touch;
Please continue to touch my heart and
my hand—
For at first you were momma…Now
You're also my husband.

I accept this Lord—If this is Your Will…
For in my heart I shall be very still;
For I know in my heart, You are
definitely a Friend,
And in this relationship…I don't have to
pretend.

Lord there are times when I do get sad,
Yet there are times when I am glad;
I am glad when I—Give You my
problems,
Because I realize Lord…That only You
can solve them.

**So please Lord- Once again, I say
thanks,
For solving my problems- I know I
can't;
Thank You for being there again and
again,
Thank You, also, for being my Best
Friend!!!**

<u>I Am Still Alone</u>

Oh Lord hear my plea—and listen to my
heart,
I feel so alone…like we're a million
miles apart.
My heart is at such a low—there's even
an emptiness in my chest,
My mind is in such confusion—Oh, Lord
what a mess.

My life—my heart—my mind—Lord, I
feel so alone,
Even though there's others present…in
my blessed home.
It's so very hard to give of myself—For I
hate being rejected,
I know if I ran for an office—I'd never
be elected.

Because I feel no one cares fore me—For
I'm as worthless as a penny
If I gave of my time—myself—no one
would want any,
Of my love, my life, my heart, my time
or my home,
Oh Lord please help me right now...***For
I am still alone!!!!!***

****

<u>Praise God</u>

Praise God everyone...with all your
soul,
Praise the Lord with all of your might;
Praise Him For the things He has done,
Praise Him for strength...His
Son...Your sight.

Praise God for the earth…stars and the moon,
Praise My Lord for the rising sun;
Praise Him for families, friends and health,
Praise God for everything "He's" done.

<u>Jesus</u>

Jesus, **I love You** with my heart mind and soul;
Jesus, I love you more than silver and gold.

Jesus, You mean so very much to me;
Jesus, You're Everything…All that I need!

Jesus, You're my mother—giving me true Love,
You're also my Father—Here on earth and above.

Jesus, You provide me with so many things,
<u>*Jesus,*</u> **You are my *EVERYTHING!***

<u>Our Children: God's Love From Above</u>

Children are definitely gifts from God.
They are expressions of His Love;
Each one of us came first this way,
From my Lord, God…up above.

As children, we were so innocent,
Born unaware of right from wrong;
But as we grew we learned prejudice,
Through TV—books and songs.

We learned to dislike and be against,
Things we could not understand
ourselves;
We raised our children in different ways,
Pointing some of them straight to hell!!!

Now we need to seek God's assistance
in—
Giving our Children what thy need;
So, since our children came from God up
above,
***We can depend on His
Love......Indeed!!!***

So parents let's get our act together,
Let's point our children to God's Love;
Because they are expressions of His
Love anyway,
***And God's Love is a "Gift" from
above!!!***

<u>Let God's Will Be Done</u>

God's Will for me in this life
Takes precedence over mine;
If you were smart you'd reprioritize,
Your life…while there is still time.

So many times we think we know
What's best for us in this life!
But I'm here to state without a doubt,
God's Will can diminish strife.

Strife in this sense…Just follow Him
Do this no matter what the course:
'Cause recalling the damage when I was
in charge—
I realize ***"WITH GOD I HAVE NO***
REMORSE".

I had been my own captain for too long.
As a result I experienced much dismay;
But now that I'm following God's Will
for me,
I've never seen brighter days.

God's Love

REJOICE!!! REJOICE!!! *God loves you and me!*
This one thing you need never doubt.
Even when you experience adversities,
God's Love will bring you out.

I know a great deal about His Love,
I have encountered it through the years;
God has expressed His Love in His Word
To be heard by spiritual ears!

So the next time you try to challenge His Love…
And want to know, "God, Why have You left me?'
Just listen to God's Spirit in your heart,
Saying **"Servant, I'll never leave thee."**

<u>Lord, I Owe It All To You</u>

Lord, You mean so much to me…
More than I could ever express:
I could never thank You enough,
'Cause I have truly been blessed!

How could I every repay You Lord,
For the blessings You have given;
I want to serve You each and every day,
While I am in the land of the living!

Oh Lord, please let me render to You
My heart, my mind, my soul!
I want to give all of me to You…
Lord, please…please…make me whole.

Lord, You have been a mother to me,
When You took my earthly mother
home;
You've even been my Father and
Savior—
Lord, You've never left me alone!

So please my LORD…Stay with me.
Always be right by my side!
And maintain a need inside my soul
To have You to always abide.

<u>Hope</u>

Hope is the faith to believe in something,
It carries one thru disbelief;
It comforts one's mind through certain
crisis,
And gives once a sense of relief!

Hope tends to keep one holding on,
To life, to joy, to love;
But let me tell you where's my hope...
My hope comes from above.

My hope comes from Jesus Christ,
He gives me an inner peace and life;
And will do the same for you,
Whatever may be your strife!!!!

<u>I Need You Lord, In My Life</u>

I need You Lord in my life,
My heart holds You very dear;
I can't imagine a day without You,
I need for You to be near.

Near me Lord all through the day,
Whether I'm asleep or awake;
Whether I 'm on the road or at home,
I need You for my heart's sake.

You see my heart can't function,
Without knowing You are near;
I've been that way all my life,
Because Your Presence is very Dear!!!

So Yes, I need You in my life,
Lord please don't You ever leave me;
Oh Lord I hate just to think,
Of living without You close to me.

<u>The Keys to My Life</u>

Jesus holds the main **Keys** to my life,
He's the only One who can get in…
Into my soul, my heart, my mind,
My thoughts and even penetrates my
skin.

I chose the **Master Key** one day,
When I found out that He Loved me;
He gave me peace—inner joy…and
Spiritual eyes to let me see!

I see His wonderful and glorious power
As He works in my daily life;
Now having Him in my heart,
Gives me joy and peace…not strife!

**So, You see why He holds the Keys to
my life,**
He's the best decision I've ever made;
*I would never exchange these "Keys" to
my life*
***For all the earthly riches…No, I would
never trade!***

9-23-93

Dear Leonard;

How are you feeling? Fine I hope. Just a few lines to let you know that I really do love you! I pray that you love me too.

I am very glad that you are feeling better. I realize that you were very sick last week. I thank God for healing you. Just don't try to do anything too soon. Take your time.

I know that sometimes things do not go as we would like for them to go, but just be patient. Let's continue to put our trust in the Lord. He will make everything alright. Anyway, He knows what is best. He always has our best interest in mind.

Love always,
Brenda

<u>Rules of Love</u>

Reassure me when I'm afraid; Miss me
when I'm away—
Keep good the vows that you made;
Believe in what I say.
Laugh with me when I'm happy; and cry
with me when I'm blue…
And when you love me, really love me—
Prove your love is true.

Correct me when I'm wrong; Stand by
me when I'm right—
Think of me in the morning and dream of
me at night;
**Just follow me to the ends of the
earth—As I would follow you.**
Love me with all your heart…**And keep
our young love true!**

Kiss me softly and gently—hold me
gently, but tight—
And if I should lose my temper...Please
don't let us fight!
When you say love me—Mean it with all
your heart,
*And if you really mean it—Oh! Even
death can't make us part!*

Forgive me when I'm not myself, try to
understand—
Just put your strong arms around me and
tightly hold my hand:
Believe in the way I do—when I expect
you to;
**There's nothing in this world that can
take away my trust in you.**

God Bless you when you say your
prayers—the way I pray for
you...
And tell "Him" Oh! with all your soul, to
keep our young love true;
**Keep these rules with everything that
you have to give...**
**Though rules that are made are
sometimes broken—*Our love was made
TO LIVE!!!!!!!!!!!!!!!***

Brenda Linton (your wife)

<u>Loneliness</u>

When you are there with no one to share,
All of those long and wondering
thoughts—
Then it is time for you to look for that
lost dream,
The one which you at once sought!

You may have looked here and there—In
fact everywhere,
Until you had given up all hope and
desire;
And then one day when you looked in
"your mirror",
You saw something there which was
once admired.

****

64

<u>Reach Out and Touch Someone Today</u>

Reach out and touch some one today,
Tell them you care before it's too late.

Reach out and touch someone right now,
This will help you both—And How!

Reach out and touch someone's hand,
Take a walk together across this land;

Reach out and touch someone new,
Therefore no one would ever get blue.

Reach out and touch someone today,
This will bring about a brighter day!!!!!

<u>Why???</u>

Why am I so lonely and blue?
Why don't I have anything to do?
Why am I all by myself?
As if there's no one in this world left?

Why do I have to eat alone?
Why is this house not a home?
Why do I cry myself to sleep?
Why is it that nightly I weep?

Why can't I have someone to love?
Why can't I be as happy as a dove?
Why can't I be held tight?
Why do I feel all alone at night?

Why have I been so deprived?
Of things that bring joy to my eyes…
This joy comes in the shape of a
husband,
Who can also love me and be my biggest
fan?

What's Your Hang Up Besides the Telephone?

Every night at 6:00
I hear the telephone ring;
Without a doubt—It will be...
John Doe doing his thing!

The voice I hear—is very soft,
And apologizing with ease;
Without reservation he constantly asks me,
If I am at all busy.

After all the petty talk is over,
And we begin to conversationalize;
I guess we talk without hesitation,
Finding enjoyment—we didn't realize.

He's usually at work when he calls,
Which he enjoys quite well;
Because he always has something,
About his job to tell!

He is trying to reach the top,
To become a manager in two years;
I wish him all the best in the world
And pray that nothing interferes!

But when he does reach the top,
Of this management race:
I wonder what will be there…
To continue his life hood pace?

What will he seek after then?
This decision he has not made;
But whatever it is, I do hope
His dues in life have been paid!

<u>Why Am I Here?</u>

In the beginning 'was mom and dad'
Who got together one night;
They tossed and rolled all around,
But believe me it was no fight!

They loved each other very much,
Which they displayed in each embrace;
Then all at once…it happened,
I arrived nine months late.

Now I am here all alone,
In this dark and lonely room;
Tell me why am I here…
One thousand years too soon?

Why am I here in this world?
Of Hate…Loneliness…and Distrust?
I'm sure there is happiness somewhere,
Away from this world of lust!

So someone…anyone…please tell me,
What is my purpose here?
Because life for me is a living hell,
Giving me no time for joy or cheer!

<u>I Need Someone To Love</u>

Loving someone is something,
Being in love is something else;
Please, who am I in Love with
Of the opposite sex!

The one I really loved,
Is with me no more;
Now living…day to day to day,
Is a headache and a chore!

I think about him all the time…
I pray for him to the One above;
But I realize that I must forget,
The one in whom I was in love.

I'm trying to live a normal life,
Going out and meeting new friends;
Please God, My Lord, help me,
To fall in love again!

I'm not choosy—He needn't be
handsome,
He need not even be wealthy;
All I ask from him is to…
Be in love with me and healthy!

<u>Could I Survive In Marriage?</u>

**Could I survive in marriage...with all
its obligations?**
If I really wanted to—I'd show complete
dedication!

I'd love you, my husband always...and
cherish your position;
I would grant your most "every"
desire...even cooking in the kitchen.

I'd nurse you when you're sick...and
bring you back to health—
For your health next to our love—means
more to me than any wealth.

I'll cook your favorite foods—each and
every day,
I'd keep the house all tidied...no matter
what others say!

We'll have children when you want—
we'll name one after you;
***There wouldn't be anything…for you I
wouldn't do.***

Sure we'll have some arguments…and
some disagreements,
But what is that compared to—our love
and earthly achievements?

***<u>So you ask me again, my darling—
"Could I survive in marriage with
you?"
I'll repeat this one more time—"Sure
darling, and you can too!!"</u>***

Love,
Brenda

<u>**Free To Love**</u>

Darling I love you with all of my heart,
My desire is that we never depart;
Because you mean so very much to me,
Without your love…*I would never be free.*

Fre*e to love you darling…*To give and to receive,
Without your love…my heart would surely freeze!!!!!
Freeze…Become cold…LOVE ME…Before it is too late!
Show me that you love me…Being your help-mate!

My darling...please...please...listen to me!
Let both of our hearts...always be free;
Free to dwell forever in each others lives...
Free to belong to each other...until the day we die!

Love,
Your Wife,

Brenda Linton

<u>Until You Walked Into My Life</u>

Life was once a great big drag,
I had allowed myself to become a hag;
I didn't like anyone—including myself...
I didn't want companionship—and no
other help.

I worked and worked and took care of
the kids...
I had no social life—work was all I did;
I also drowned myself in the TV,
So work, children, and TV—was the
whole world to me.

I was always angry—angry at
everyone...I would never go out—
Dating I would shun;
Life for me was a great big bore,
To even talk to anyone was a great big
chore.

Then you came along, and sat at the
table,
I knew at one glance that I would be
able—
To give, to share, to give you my heart to
love,
I thought you were sent from the man
above.

Well, you know the story—I asked you
the time...
For one moment I thought I committed a
crime;
A crime of approaching you...Which I
never did before!
But our hour-long conversation...Just
opened up the door.

Opened the door—of my heart—my life,
I felt better about you—than when I was
a wife;
A wife to someone else in the past years,
In the short time we talked, I felt I could
cheer!!!

Hip, hip hooray...for this wonderful
guy...
Who was nice to be with—but extremely
shy;
But under that shy and quiet "hunk of a
being",
I knew for once I was finally seeing!

Seeing beauty, love and all the wonderful
things,
That life really holds for all human
beings;
So now since you've walked right into
my life,
I couldn't love you anymore—If I were
your wife!

BRENDA

<u>Our Daily Walk</u>

Please don't get upset with me,
If we differ in our thoughts;
Because we may be at different levels,
In our daily walk!

You may decide at this very moment,
That you may want to go one way;
Do ahead…please…do your thing—
But please baby…Let me have my say.

'Cause no two people will think alike,
Or agree on every single thought:
Whether born as triplets, twins or
separately—
We all differ in our daily walk!

Brenda Martin

<u>Darling, I Do Love You!!!</u>

It's (time), (date),—And I'm writing to
you,
Because my heart has so much to say:
My feelings for you darling just keep
growing,
Each and every passing day!

It's hard to explain just how I feel,
Because my heart is about to burst:
But burst it can…this good feeling
Of love—Of life…Of thirst!

Thirst for the touch of your masculine
hands,
As we hold hands and we kiss:
Thirst for the squeeze of your powerful
arms,
That for years I ran and missed.

But I'm not sorry at the least,
For those six years I ran from you;
'Cause it just makes our love stronger,
As it keeps our love young and true!

It's funny that things happened…this
way,
I guess we ran long enough…
To run "smack dab" into each other,
Which makes our wonderful love **tough!**

Too tough to break…bringing us closer,
To each others as we should be;
I pray that you're as happy as I,
For next to God, I pray you do love me!

I'm praying to my Lord and Savior,
That He blesses our new found love:
I want His seal of approval,
To descend to us from above!

**For without His consent, We love in
vain—
And our feelings will definitely pass;
So I pray that you are praying for the
same,
So our love can <u>last</u> and <u>last</u>!**

I pray that our love is always exciting
As it is every time we meet;
Because I don't know how my love is to
you,
But your love to me is "so sweet".

There's one thing darling, I must boldly
say…
You render me speechless with your
gentle touch:
I can't move, speak or even express
Not only my love…But how much!!!

I pray so much…50 years from now,
That I still melt from your every touch:
It's a feeling I possess only for you,
And I treasure it very much…

So darling I close with these tender
words,
From my heart darling…And they are
true;
I can *whisper*, **YELL or S C R E A
M…*Out loud*,**
<u>**"Yes Leonard, I DO LOVE
YOU!!!!!!"**</u>

Love,
Tour wife,

Brenda J. Linton

<u>To My "Daddy" Leonard—My Husband to Be</u>

This morning Leonard, the Lord woke me up... With the love for you in my heart;
I prayed to my Lord and Savior, Jesus Christ...**That we will never part.**

After I thanked the Lord for waking me up...I thought about the dream I had last night
Love just happens when one least expects it...Darling, your presence makes my heart chime.

Daddy I realize we have both experienced a divorce...A divorce—in the past;
I just pray that our love can overcome our losses...**I pray that our love last and last!**

You see, ***since we've come into each other's life...*** I have begun to laugh more and more;
You've brought back to me laughter in my soul...Yes, Leonard, it's you now I adore.

And as your wife, I would love you both day and night…I'll listen to you as you talk; Yes, I'll be your "*helpmate*" as God states…By your side Leonard, gladly I will walk!!!

But we cannot act as husband and wife now…We must and will do it God's way; No matter how we try to rationalize…**We must listen to and obey what God says!**

We must go to church…listen to God's way…Always works out for the best; I speak this as a personal testimony…Yes, in doing this—I have always been blest!

We must go to church…**listen to God's Word**…Understand God's meaning of 'one'— Then & only then can our love be expressed**…**That obligation to our Lord must be done!

You find out in life that doing things god's way…Always works out for the best; I speak this as a personal testimony…Yes, in doing this—I have always been blessed!!!

As your wife I'll be there whenever you
want...I'll be honored walking by your side;
**'Cause with your strong arms around
me'**...In your care—I will lovingly abide.

I'll pray for you to handle my love with
care...And handle my body as your heart's
treasure;
For if you keep my care in your heart...**Our
love will grow beyond measure!**

*I realize we have difference in
opinion*...Regarding some matter that we have
discussed;
But that's okay sweetheart, as long as...talk
about them loving—& not fuss!!!

We should & would never let anything. Come
between out love we have for each other
**God states when you marry, 'cling to one
another'**...My heart can think of nothing
better.

You see, with, I never want to fight...Leonard,
I would feel better just loving you;
We already know you are **quite physically
strong**...So your tenderness with me will do.

Your tenderness will make desire to do…As
the Lord has given wives in a list;
**One of these things that the Lord has
stated…*Is for the wife to her
husband*…Submit!**

Leonard, I have no problems with this…For
God tells husbands o give their wife protection;
Believe me, I'll love this position of
submission…I'll look to you for leadership &
direction.

Direction as to what's best for me…For I pray
that you consult with the Lord above;
In all of the decisions for our lives…**For God
assigned husbands** to lead and show love.

*I believe in encouraging my God—given
husband*…**Leonard,** I take no back seat to this;
Just remember though—I am a person. So
rather than argue -please let us kiss!

Let us kiss & discuss the matter at hand…But
please always deal with me with your heart;
Because darling, if you always treasure me
there…**Our love will never from us depart!!!**

Darling Leonard let me add this little note...As
we consider our future plans;
That you never consider dealing with me/With
the blow of your strong hands

For we already know of your great
strength...There's only one way to apply it on
me;
That's when you caress me in your arms/ And
hold me ever—so tenderly.

**That's the only time I'll accept the
fall**...Because your touch will render my knees
weak;
I will then depend on your strong hands...
**Your strong arms "Daddy"...my body will
seek.**

Let us always be—be pals and friends...This is
the way our relationship began;
We started out trusting outs hearts to each
other...Let's not allow this loyalty to end!!!

So as I close Leonard, I just want to say…*Our love is definitely a blessings form Christ;* Daddy, with God's Blessing I'll be honored…**To be Your Help Mate…Lover…YOUR WIFE!!!** *(sometime in the future)* Love—Forever & Always, Brenda Martin

As My Husband/Man/…You Must Spoil Me!!!!!

<u>**Spoil me—you must Leonard—for I am "Your Lady"**</u>…This act I expect you to do;
For to spoil me—Makes my 'soul rejoice' don't fret—
I'm gonna love spoiling you too!

In a marriage relationship…when two people
unite…There's a union of mind, body & soul;
For both will always want to be so close…That instead
of two people we'll make one whole!!!

In seeing two as one, because of the "bond…It's such a
good feeling of love and desire;
That to spoil one another at all times…Keeps their
body, mind and soul on fire!!!

Also with this union—there's such a bond I can't
express…There's such loyalty and strong ties;
That one person can't fall without the other…If one is
sad the other one cries!!!

But even before we crisis that 'marriage' bridge,
Leonard…*I can still be spoiled by you;*
For I love cards and flowers, and plenty of
attention…***Spoiling me should be a pleasure to do!!!***

Ah Shucks!!, Leonard I love to spoil you as well,
Times I write you a poem or a song;
"Cause there's some things only my heart can
relate…To the man that will share our home!"

Oh, Leonard, just spoil me, What's there to loose:
This I may write you a poem or a song;
'Cause there's some things only my heart can
relate…To the man that will share our home!!!

**Oh Leonard, just spoil me, What's there to
lose…**This is the easiest task you'll ever have;
And if spoiling you makes you glad—Then I
Must…**Spoiling each other will express our love!!!**

Just keep on opening car doors for me…And continue
to take me on dates;
For we have to share some times together…Before we
become 'help mates'!!!

Oh Leonard, just spoil me—<u>DON'T COMPLAIN</u>…It
should bring great pleasure to you;
For you should be honored to spoil me darling…**I'm
certainly going to enjoy spoiling you!!!**

*You can still be yourself, Leonard, while spoiling
me…*Just keep me happy as your wife;
You'll see that's one secret of a happy marriage…**For
it brings joy & eliminates strife!!!**

**Don't worry you're too strong in your own personality...*To allow me to take control;*
But spoiling me won't put me in charge...It'll just keep me loving your "soul"!!!**

I know you're the man—I have no problem with this...For I believe you are just what I need;
So don't feel threatened when I ask for attention...**As your wife, I need you to lead!!!**

In fact, I don't want to have charge in marriage...That's the position God assigned to you;
I just want to be kept happy by my husband...I definitely do not want to wear your shoes!

Spoiling each other—whatever it takes...Even switching roles in the kitchen or in the yard;
Love has no barriers in "God's Marriage...to heed to this will be wise and quite smart!!!

And if spoiling each other brings us joy...I think it'll be time for us to 'then' to yield;
'Cause if any 2 people are deserving—IT'S US...From our divorces—Our hearts need to heal!!!

Our hearts need to heal—this is what we need...For we have suffered enough in our hearts;
So I'll spoil you Leonard—and you'll spoil me...I can think of no better role or part!!!

But we cannot begin to meet the challenge…Of
spoiling or meeting each other's needs;
"Cause Leonard you must get your act together…So
our lives together—can be set free!!!

<u>**Set free to live as husband & wife**</u>…*Leonard our
souls must be set free;*
Free to express every part of our lives…**So hurry
up—so your life includes me!!!**

'Cause although I'm 41 and mature…When I see
you—I feel like putty in your hands;
That's why I tell you not to come within 10 feet of
me…<u>**For I must maintain my stand!!!**</u>

*It's getting so when we're on the phone…You render
me helpless in my mind and heart;
"Leonard, what are you doing to me?"…You could do
no more harm if I were in your arms!"*

So Leonard, I can't hardly wait to be spoiled by
you…***Just spoil me until I scream—
'Cause I know I'm gonna love spoiling you…***
<u>**When we become a God-given ONE…MAN
TEAM!!!**</u>

Love always,
Brenda Martin

Baby, Your Love Is…

Baby your love is so doggone strong…You made love to me right over the phone;
When I called in on my answering machine,
Your strong sexy voice started doing its thing.

Oh! You did not really say very much…
But for each word…I could feel your touch;
All over me…*"Oh! I felt so good,"*
Like a woman in love—could and should!!!

Your words were ***soft, short and sweet…***
Just like they were when we first did meet;
But what gets me honey, is what you do,
When all you say is **"Baby, I love you"**!!!

Well please the next time…*when you call—*
Be willing to catch me when I fall;
Because your voice makes me so dog-gone weak,
That I get buckled knees and unsteady feet.

But I don't mind it…coming from you,
Because our love is so "very, very true"
So call me again…anytime you desire—
<u>Just tell me you love me and set my soul on fire!!!!!</u>

Love,
Your wife,

Brenda Linton

"Listen Leonard, Get Your Act Together!"

Listen, Leonard, *let's make this place a home,*
I'm tired of "courting" on the telephone;
When I want to talk just to you,
I'm tired of going thru a person or two.

Now enough is enough, let's hurry up,
I'm tired of this "waiting stuff";
Now you want me and I want you,
So let us do what we have to do!

Since you have come into my empty life,
I've felt like a person, your friend...Your
potential wife;
You've been like a "husband to be" to me,
The only thing missing is "I do wed thee."

I know we're making these wonderful plans,
We can't do anything about a loving romance;
I can't allow things to get out of hand,
**So let's hurry up and get married...So that
we can.**

It is my desire for us never to make,
A mistake to get from under Gods grace...
So please Leonard—I'm not rushing things,
But I know what our kind of relationship can
bring!

I realize there are steps to take,
And many wedding plans we have to make;
But listen darling, **"I do love you,"**
And we know the proper thing to do.

So let us ask God to bless our love,
And send His blessed approval from above;
But let's do "HIS WILL" And not burn,
By our love...Let matrimony take it's turn.

Your Wife -To- Be,

Brenda J. Martin

The First Time: A Need to Flee

The first time I ever saw you,
I ran for my soul survival;
Because I knew if I "tangled" with you,
I would need more than a revival!

The first time you gazed into my eyes,
I knew I had better flee;
Because to be that close to you,
Was a great disaster for me!

The first time I allowed you
To kiss me on the cheek—
I said, "Go Leonard…Run away"
Because my knees were getting too weak.

The very first time I permitted
For you to hold my hand,
I knew at that very moment,
To run while I could still stand!

The first time that you held me (about 5 1/2
years later)
It was too much for me to take;
So I pushed you away, and hurriedly left,
For to stay would have been a mistake!

So you see the first time for everything,
With you—Caused me to flee indeed;
Because you were too much for me,
<u>**You were what I wanted—not need!!!!!**</u>

Love,
Your Wife,

Brenda Linton

<u>With God We Can Be Certain</u>

So many times in my lonely life,
I've asked my God above;
"Please send someone to care about me,
Yes, send me someone to love!!!"

This request had become a part of me-
It had almost passed my soul:
For I know me...And God knows too,
I just needed someone to hold.

Someone to hold in my loving arms,
Someone to possess my tender heart:
God knows I wanted the kind of love,
That would cause us to never part!

I wanted this love to result in making
That God-Giving commitment of a vow;
So now the time grows closer and closer,
***The uncertainty is surmounting*—and how!**

Oh! I love being with this dear strong man,
I love him dearly—For there is no doubt;
But will this love hold for the many years,
Or will our differences make us shout!

Shout at each other—rather than talk,
Or remain silent—for long periods of time;
I want the lines of communication to always be
open,
Let our anger commit no sinful crimes.

Crimes against God—We must not do
that—
We must never deny one another;
We must cling to each other no matter what,
And turn deaf ear to meddling brothers.

We must be able to weather the storm—
To keep God as the head of our lives;
If we remember the aforementioned
precautions,
Certainty with God will keep us as husband
and wife!

Jesus Help Me Make it Through These Lonely Nights Tribute to My Lord and Savior

At this very moment, loneliness fills my heart,
For I feel all alone…Please Jesus don't You
from me part;
***I need your loving arms to hold me very
tight…***
**Please Dear Jesus, help me make it through
these lonely nights.**

These last few nights, I tossed and turned, a
great deal through the night,
When I did fall asleep, nightmares kept me in
much fright:
*Again, Lord, I am alone, but I need something
from you*
Now that my husband has gone home, ***Lord I
will still need you!***

This loneliness Lord, really hearts…It tears at
my very soul,
Lord I had companionship…now I am all
alone:

I need, You Lord to be with me…and for You
to love me too…
Although Leonard is gone on home…I know I
will still need you.

Please don't let me cry myself…to sleep
again tonight,
Draw me in your tender arms my Lord, and
please cuddle me tight:
Please don't turn your back on me- Lord, to
me, remain true
Because Lord there's no comfort if…I'm not
loved by you.

*So, please Lord understand- Love is a great
need,*
For to love and to be loved back is one way to
be free;
*Free from the loneliness- that will escalate at
night,*
**<u>Please, Lord Jesus help me make it through
these many lonely nights.</u>**

Your Child and Servant,

Brenda Linton

<u>Happy Valentine's Day Leonard, My Darling Husband</u>

Leonard, my sweet and darling husband
I love you with all my heart
I pray to the Lord almighty Jesus
That we shall never part.

The Lord knew what we both needed.
He continued to prepare us year by year;
That's why our love is so special
And in my heart, you are so dear!

Our getting together in marriage
Is surely a blessing from above...
I knew then and I know now,
That our Lord is in charge of our love!

So I'd like to say to you Leonard
On this Valentines Day in 1994
If you searched from now until eternity,
You'd find no one who could love you more.

And I pray that you feel the same,
About your love you possess for me;
Because with God…you and me in love
Could last an e-ter-ni-ty!!!

So my final prayer for our love is this;
That our relationship will never cease:
However…God's love for the both of us
Without a doubt will continue to be…

Love,
Your Wife,

<u>Happy Valentine's Day, Jesus;</u>
<u>1995</u>

A Valentine's card I wrote to my husband,
Leonard…In '94—He was also my friend;
However, 2 weeks later—My Lord and
Savior…Brought Leonard's earthly life to its end.

In that card I expressed my love for Leonard…Indeed
Leonard—was sent from above;
Now 1 year later since that Valentine's season…I'm
writing to Jesus—**<u>My Heavenly Valentine Love!</u>**

I'm not afraid of You leaving me, Jesus…For You are
My Lord and Creator:
I love You and You Love me dearly…**You are indeed
my Eternal Savior.**

Even though this heart of mine still grieves…For the
great love that Leonard and I shared:
The Love I possess for You, ***<u>My Lord and Savior</u>***…Is
Love that is beyond compare!!!

On this Valentines Day of 19-95, Jesus…I know
without a doubt in my heart—
That the Love you and I have for each other…Shall
Never—Never—Nev—er part!!!

Brenda J. Martin-Linton

This love that is shared with You, alone, Lord…Is
Love…beyond the grave…
For You lived…died…and rose to set me free…Yes
my Lord—my soul You have saved!!!

Saved from death…Yet, saved unto You…Saved from
damnation and hell-fire…
The **Love** expressed in "Your Death" for me…Makes
You my Heavenly and Eternal Desire!!!

I love You Lord—For You first **Loved** me…Now
You're my Husband, Friend and Mate:
I'm so glad to have You as my Valentine's Partner—
On this 19-95 Valentine's date!!!

**Lord, continue to Love me and fill my soul—My
spirit—my mind—and my heart…**
For I know with this Love that We share together…It
will Never—Never—Nev-er depart!

I rest in these facts; That You'll forever Love me…I
know You'll never leave me alone;
For You are My Lord My Savior—& My God…Even
when I die…Your Love will take me home!

So again I say, "***Happy Valentine's Day, Jesus***—Yes,
it's so wonderful to be alive…**
Yes its great to be rocked in Your Bosom of
Love…*Happy Valentine's Day Jesus…of 19—95!!*"

**_Love,_
Brenda Martin -Linton**

Rest Leonard: God's Darling Child

(I wrote and read it for his funeral)
(He went to live with Lord on Wednesday, February 23,1994)

Tribute to Leonard

Rest, Leonard: God's Darling Child...God
has released your earthly fears;
And My Lord and Savior Christ...Has
drawn you very near.

There is no need to fret anymore...For
you're now laying in God's Strong Arms;
In God's loving way—He decided to
take...You from all earthly harm.

He has dried your tear stained eyes...He has
relaxed you from all unease;
He has stilled your loving and tender
heart...He has fulfilled all of your needs.

So you placed, that night, your tired weary
head...Gently on God's tender chest;
I know that there is no earthly
comfort...That compares to that peaceful
rest.

<u>Yes, my darling love you will be missed</u>...*By
me and others* who are still here;
But the Beauty of this eternal rest Leonard,
God's Love Child...Is the absence of all
fears!!!

So again...rest my husband, God's Darling
Child...Your earthly pain is forever gone:
For you're in the bosom of my Lord and
Savior...***<u>Leonard, you're in Your Heavenly
Home!!!</u>***

Your Beloved Wife
Brenda Linton
I Shall Always Love you Leonard

The Finale Letter

The Silenced Footsteps

The footsteps of yours Leonard, My husband and Lover,
Brought much love and joy to my heart;
But now your foot steps have been silenced because
Your love and life from me have depart!!!

Your footsteps made my fluttering heart leap;
I smiled every time you walked through the door;
But my Lord and Savior, Jesus Christ
Received you…because He loved you more!

I never believed anyone could ever love you, Leonard,
As much as I did…within my soul;

However, my Lord rocked your soul gently in
His arms
And left your body here…stiff and cold.

**I almost lost my mind that February night
When I found you in your eternal sleep;**
But as time passes, I 'm trying to remember
Our souls are not ours to keep.

Our souls belong to my Lord and Savior—
Our life here is only a loan;
For after this brief stay here on earth,
We must go to our eternal home.

**<u>Yet, your death has left a gigantic void,
In my heart…Yes, my heart has been
shattered!!!</u>**
Yet, I must remember, my life must continue
For with you Leonard, my happiness is all that
mattered.

Yes, my darling Leonard, while alive you
would give to me,
With a smile…The shirt off your back!!!
You state to me on numerous occasions,
"Brenda, for your happiness I will take the
slack."

Yes, I must accept this inevitable fact...
Of your silenced footsteps in my life;
For now I'm the bride of Jesus Christ,
And no longer an earthly wife!

But in my heart, Leonard, you still live;
You are part of my very soul;
However, for now our lives have been
separated,
Yet, our love remains as pure as gold.

So even though your footsteps have been
silenced, Leonard...
Your Love still screams in my heart;
Besides my love, for my Lord, Jesus Christ,
and our children,
Your love shall never from me
depart!!!!!!!!!!!!!!!!!!!!!!!!!!!!!

Love forever and ever
Your wife,

Brenda J. Linton

<u>A Wife's Request For Understanding:</u> <u>To Leonard (Now at Home with the Lord)</u>

The tear's don't stop—They just continue to drop…To flow
Emotions remain confused…Not knowing whether to stop or go;
This house ***screams out Leonard…***It **shouts** your very name!!!
The days just come and go—But my deep love for you remains.

That love—only you Leonard—Looked deep enough to see:
That love that you gave…And set my soul a-free;
That love that just a look from you…Could calm me quietly down—
That love—with your smile…Would make me never want to frown!!!!!

Your love—your smile... Would brighten my
darkest day—
Your love—your touch—Could make my tired
body want to play;
Your love—your touch, Leonard...Would
make my body ***SCREAM!!!!!***
**Your love—your touch, Darling...Made us a
one man's team.**

Your touch—your love...Always set my soul
a-fire
Your love—your smile...Made you my one
man desire;
Your touch—your love...Made my heart
scream and shout!!!
Yes, "you" Leonard—was what...Leonard was
all about.

So now you know why your touch... Would
always make me cry—
And why your warm smile...Made me want to
live...Not to die;
But now your smiles and touches...Are forever
out of my life—
But even these memories make it an
Honor...To have been your wife!!!

I think of all the things… That you wanted to
give to me—
Your only crime in our life together… **Was to
make, Leonard, "Happy"!!!!!**
You had a continuous desire to buy
me…Silver—cars and gold—
But then—even now—I only need your love
and understanding…This is for my very soul!!!

Now I confess—I learned from you…Marriage
is indeed a great joy:
That's why God turned you into "My
Man"…From a "little boy".
You made "our marriage" a great need…As
well as our desire—
For our marriage was a union… **That set our
souls on fire!!!!!**

***Darling, marriage—was our bond…It set our
souls—FREE!!!***
Though we appeared to join as two—
Including Our Lord made us three:
By that I mean—though we joined hands…Our
Lord—was there too:
***To consummate "our bond"…That's what
Our God wanted us to do!!!!!***

With this spiritual binding present in our
marriage...It's so hard living here alone-
For Leonard when you were here...This house
was a happy home;
Now this deafening silence...Leonard, I can no
longer stand—
Leonard, once again—I need someone...*To
hold this lonely hand.*

At one time—before we met...I prayed "Lord
Jesus, please send
A mate—a friend—a lover to me...In the form
of "A Wonderful Husband!!!!!"
God answered my prayer—Yes, indeed...He
sent "My Darling"—YOU—
But now Leonard—You've gone Home with
Our Lord...*We are no longer—"2"!!!*

So please Leonard—understand...Why I'm
going to God—again:
For a new mate—A friend—a partner...For a
new husband.
For once again I am by myself...And it's no
good being here alone—
I need someone here with me...*I want this
house returned to "a home"!!!!*

I know this about you Leonard, "My
Love"…That you do understand:
Why again I'm asking Our Lord…For a new
earthly husband;
For my happiness was always #1…"On your
earthly chart"—
**But no matter who God sends,
Leonard…I'll always love you in my
heart!!!**

GOOD-BYE—SLEEP ON LEONARD, MY DARLING—I'LL SEE YOU IN HEAVEN!!!

LOVE ALWAYS, Your Wife

Brenda

Dedications

Dedicated to My Lord and Savior Jesus Christ, who is the head of my life, my wonderful husband Leonard, my daughters April and Isis, and to all my Christian brothers and sisters whom I have come in contact with through my Christian Walk.

Brenda J. Martin-Linton

<u>Dedication: To The Pastor</u>

To the Pastor and his wife Lorraine,
Who walks in the footsteps of God!
I pray that one day I can follow
To places where you may trod!

I met you both three years ago,
When the Lord led me to Grace Church;
Ever since I've been in the fold,
I've been taught that I do have worth.

To the Pastor and his wife Lorraine,
You've been two easy people to love;
Because whatever you say about the Lord,
Has God's blessings' from above.

With the both of you...one can talk and
cry...
You are sure to give God's advice;
I can say this truly as a matter of fact,
'Cause I've done it once or twice!

So I dedicate this poem to the both of you!
I thank God for sending you
Because so far what you've told me
Lets me know to God, you're true.

Brenda J. Martin-Linton

So please celebrate many more years,
Giving service to My Lord!!!!!!!
Because the celebration of other things,
Will reap no spiritual reward!!!

<u>Isis: My Love Child</u>

Isis, you are my special love child,
You are very dear to me;
You have a way about yourself,
That holds "to my heart" a key.

A key that unlocks your feelings,
And relates them to how I may feel;
You definitely keep my ideas fresh,
And you've taught me when to yield.

Yes, you've had your problems,
Just as any young child would;
But there's one thing that I learned is,
You strive to do just what you should.

It was you that I always held so—
Close to my heart each night;
That's why it's so difficult for me,
To let you out of my sight.

***So forgive me Isis my love child,
If while you try to snip the cord;
That I'm the one holding on,
Because you're a gift from my dear
Lord.***

The past 12 years wasn't without
physical stress,
You had your ups and downs;
Though respiratory illness tried to plague
your youth,
You continued to smile, not frown.

Your academic climb, I must applaud,
Your accomplishments deserve much
recognition;
My darling Isis, you're done so much,
That it's more than I can mention.

So continue to display your true
happiness,
In your heart, your joy, your smile;
I know with you Isis, my love child,
We can make it for many more miles.

But even when we cease to share,
Our earthly lives with each other;
Just remember this Isis, my love child,
God will be closer than I, your mother.

Love,

Your Mom
Brenda Martin- Linton

<u>April, My Darling Child</u>

April, you brought joy to me at birth,
Even thought he pains were hard;
You smile, your love, less you had
worth,
Yes, I know you were a Gift from God.

Raising you was very new too me,
Bringing you up in the world;
But I realized then and even now,
I am blessed with you…**MY BIG
GIRL!!!**

I prayed, I laughed, I wept for you,
At different stages in your life…
But through it all, I know the Lord,
Was with you even through strife!

As I recall your youth, you nursed from
me,
I wanted the best for you…

But when you and to be abruptly
weaned,
That indeed was a hard task to do.

**You pulled...you pushed...you wanted
to nurse,
It had comforted you nine months
long;
But my darling child, to give in to you,
Would have been deadly wrong!**

I marvel at you academic climb,
That you have attained in school;
I thank God that your aptitude,
Demonstrates darling..."You are no
fool!"

*You succeeded in things...you strived
for,*
This is more than any moms' request;
I can truly say April, my sweet love,
By the Lord we have truly been blessed.

So let me give you some motherly
advice;—
April the Lord will continue to be,
With you long after we've separated—
His life with you will never cease......

<u>Love, Mom</u>

<u>B. Martin-Linton</u>

<u>Dedication—to a Married Friend</u>

You asked me. "Who are you?"
And what are you like;
I will attempt to describe you,
With all of my might.

But before I start my poem,
I would like to say to you—
Some things you may not like,
While other things you may.

Your personality—you're usually sweet and
kind,
Fun to be with...versatile and shy;
Considerate...Understanding...Even funny at
times;
Hungry for the kind of love that money can
buy!

You are not a person of very many words,
You converse more so with your eyes;
But when you decide to open your mouth...
Sometimes you tend to lie!

You try to seek much understanding-
With all of your tender heart:
But there's not much left because,
' It's been cut into so many parts.

You try so hard to be—a man of your word,
You, so many times display true dedication;
But when will you realize "married friend"
That you have enough obligations!

You want a friend of your choice,
To play a part in your daily life;
But how would you feel if when you went
home,
Someone's husband was with your wife?

Now that I have found out the truth (You told
me a lie)
That you do have a marriage obligation;
I can no longer be apart of your life,
Your wife should receive your complete
dedication!

So you ask me again, 'Who are you?'
And just what you are like;
I'll repeat without any hesitation,
You should be dedicated to your wife!

GOODBYE!!!!!!!!!!!!!

Brenda J. Martin

<u>Dedication to My Husband: Leonard</u>

It's 10:00, January 3rd—And I'm writing to
you
Because my heart has so much to say:
My feelings for you darling just keep growing,
Each and every passing day!

It's hard to explain just how I feel,
Because my heart is about to burst:
But it can…for this good feeling,
Of love—Of life…Of thirst!

Thirst for the touch of your masculine hands,
As hold hands and as we kiss:
Thirst for the squeeze of your powerful arm,
That for years I ran and missed.

But I'm not sorry at the least,
For those six years I ran from you;
'Cause it just makes our love stronger,
And it keeps our young love true.

It's funny that things happened…this way,
I guess we ran long enough…

To run "smack dab" into each other,
Which makes our wonderful love "tough".

Too tough to break…bringing us closer,
To each other as we should be;
I pray that you're as happy as I,
For next to God—I pray you do love me!

**I'm praying to My Lord and Savior,
That He blesses our new found love:**
I wanted His seal of approval,
To descend to us form above.

For without His consent, we love in vain—
And our feelings will definitely pass;
So I pray that you are praying for the same,
So our love can last and last and last.

I pray that our love is always exciting,
As it is every time we meet;
**Because I don't know how my love is to you,
But your love to me is so "sweet".**

Love forever,

Your Wife.
Brenda J. Linton

<u>Dedication to Momma: Ella Mae</u>

<u>Oh momma, Ella Mae, there's so much to say…</u>
<u>To you—who started this Bonds family.</u>
You mean so much to me in my heart…
I'm so sorry that you had to leave!!!!

Cause your presence—your sweet presence—
to all of us…
Can never be replaced…
Mom you were with me for only 35 years
Your sweet *smile* can never be erased.

**I just couldn't believe—that October '85
eve…**
Your eyes closed for the very last time.
I thought that you, mama, would live forever…
I thought that you would forever be mine!!!

I know you were sick for that period of time…
And that you were "under the weather".
*But I prayed in my heart that you would
forever live…*
I prayed you would get better!!!

But that cancer I hate it—with such a
passion…
Cause it took your young life from us.
It took your strength and vitality…
Making your exit from this life "a must"!

A must to leave because you had…
No more strength to fight this disease…
But death has no victory over your
soul…'Cause
God put your mind and soul at ease.

But I needed you, mom, you're the only mom I
knew…
It was hard to accept your death…
I need—I wanted to talk to you
Only you…though not just for myself!!!

But for all of us 5 girls—We depended on
you…
I guess that bond had to break…
But your untimely death, just like dad's
Was a pill too hard to take!!!

THIRTY FIVE YEARS MOMMA, I WANTED YOU FOREVER...

I never wanted you to die...
These last 16 years with out you here
Leaves a void—Tears in my eyes.

A void, an emptiness, a tear-stained pillow...
A loneliness only you can fill!!!
Mom, I miss you so very much...
Yes, your love is with me still.

Mom, you made that exit—you made that
crossover...
You passed from life to life
Mom you passed from life to death here on
earth...
You walked into life with **Jesus Christ!!!**

Your new life with Christ, mom brings joy to
my heart...
Though your exit brings tears to my soul...
Yet I realize that the part of your life we did
shared
Made me rich—and my spirit whole.

You brought up "us" five girls, Mom, the best
you could...
Without help because of dad's death!
But the love you provided regardless of
"lack"...
Gave us more than any monetary wealth!

Those loving things you did—helped us survive…
In this world, that we call "earth".
You gave us the tools that we would need
Like love—and a good feeling of worth.

You clothed us, protected us—gave us a home…
How you did it baffles my mind.
You worked hard to keep us fed—indeed…
Your provisions were one of a kind.

One of a kind because of how you made it…
When there was no food for us to eat.
How you went into the kitchen and whatever you did…
Food appeared—Bread, veggies and meat!!!

All I heard from the kitchen were your prayers…
And songs that praised our <u>Lord!!!</u>
Then there was a silence even I can't explain
All I know is **FOOD WE COULDN'T AFFORD!**

However- pots pans began to rattle in there.
Then aromas filled the house
Soon you would call us to the table to eat
You did all that—"without a spouse".

You did your very best in every way…
Even though you had little education…
But the love you gave us as our mother
Is one reason for this **dedication**!

***Another reason is because of your love for the
Lord…***
As I remember you praying on your knees
Always asking God, "**<u>Lord help me with my
children</u>**…
<u>**Help me provide the things they need.**</u>

"Help me to do the best I know how…
Help my baby, Brenda to get grown!!!
For when she is grown I can truly rest in peace…
I'll be ready for my heavenly home."

You see I was the baby—the last of your
children…
That you were blessed to bring in this world!
You knew that whenever—I got grown
You'll have no worry about any of "us" girls.

I couldn't understand "that" prayer—'cause I
wanted you forever…
I wanted you down here with me
**<u>So, God honored your prayers and when I
turned 35…</u>**
<u>He set your soul a-free!!!</u>

He freed you from all the cares of "this"
world…
Taking you to heaven for eternity!!!!
But mom I'm here and I miss you so much…
I wish you were still here with me.

But even though I wish for your presence
momma…
***I'm happy you're with our Lord, Jesus
Christ!!!***
'Cause being with Him is the best place to be
'Cause you now have **Eternal Life!!!**

Eternal Life is what I want too…
When I leave this life here on earth
'Cause leaving this life gives me one
assurance…
That in heaven there will be a "**NEW BIRTH**"

**A New Birth of another soul coming home
to Jesus…
A New Birth to see all my loved ones!!!
A New Birth to sing "<u>Glory Hallelujah</u>"…
A New Birth in our heavenly home!!!**

So, it's just a short time until we meet again
'cause…
A thousand years in heaven is just one day to
you
But I'm patient 'cause you'll always live in my
heart…
And mother's love is always true.

True in the heart—this love never dies…
No matter how much time spent apart.
So, though this dedication may close in pen
and paper…
Your love will always exist in my heart.

SO MOMMA KEEP PRAISING JESUS—YOU DESERVE TO BE WITH HIM…
YOU HAVE NO MORE SICKNESS TO BEAR!!!
YOU HAVE NO MORE PAIN, SORROW OR MISERY…
YOU HAVE NO MORE EARTHLY CARES!!!!

Love always,
Your baby girl…Brenda Bonds Martin-Linton

MOMMA I WILL SEE YOU AND JESUS IN HEAVEN…REST IN PEACE!!!!!!!

<u>Dedication to My Eldest Sister: Esther Lee</u>

To Esther my dear sister…The Eldest of Ella's girls
You're the best biggest sister…In this whole wide world!!!

I love you very dearly…With all of my soul and heart
Being sisters in Christ also…We shall never ever part.

You've been there for me…When I needed a hand
Giving love and assistance…Doing all that you can.

What's so great about you Sis…Is you love the Lord too
What more could one want…God truly…loves you.

You have given your life…To our Lord Jesus Christ

This gives you the assurance…*Of Everlasting Life!!!*

I'm so glad we're Christian sisters…As well as
by birth
Knowing we'll be together…When we leave
this planet earth.

We'll know our sisterhood here…Was not a
mistake
'Cause our bond together…Is more than just
great.

I believe when we see Jesus…Over in the
Promised Land
He'll say, "Look at those sisters…Walking
hand in hand!"

He'll add "I am glad that on earth…I put them
together as kin
And now here they are together…Sisters once
again."

So, in heaven when we reunite…I'll remember
your sisterly love
We'll share it in God's blessed presence…**In**
H-E-A-V-E-N above.

So, I close this dedication…But not my soul
and heart
'Cause Esther I'm so glad to know…That we
will never part.

Love,
Your baby sister,

Brenda Martin-Linton

<u>Dedication to My Christian and Blood Sister…Cora Dolly</u>

This dedication is to **Cora, my sister**…*My blood sister and sister in God above;*
God not only blessed us to share the same mother…We also share *Jesus and His great Love*!!!

My sister Cora, is very precious to me…She's a pal and a dear great friend;
She comes to my aid when I express a need…She is one in whom you can depend.

She's proven this fact, with such great love…Especially since we've become 'sisters' at Grace!
She's been there for me through my ups and downs…Yet she still allows me my space.

These ups and downs were numerous this year…With Leonard's death and my foot problem;
Cora has shown me she cares by listening to my problems…Tho' she herself couldn't solve them.

145

<u>I'm happy that the Lord has shown great favor to us</u>…**Bringing us closer in our Christian walk;**
Not only do we enjoy each other's company…We also show respect in our Christian talk!!!

Yes, there were times in our childhood years…Much time elapsed—we had no conversation;
But now the Lord is allowing us both…To grow closer in our Christian relation!!!

There may be some occasions we don't agree…But no time elapse before we're talking again:
For *Christ's Love* keep our minds tuned onto Him…He keeps us as sisters and friends!!!

My sister Cora and I are still growing in the Lord…I'm so glad we both love *Jesus Christ*:
Yes **Christ** has made a big change in our relationship…He's an inspiration in both of our lives!!!

So if you see me smiling when Cora and I are together…It's because I'm happy *Our God above*;
Has shown favor to us in our Christian walk***…To share Jesus Christ and our 'sisterly' Love!!!***

Thanks for everything…Cora
<u>With Love from your sister by birth and in Christ,</u>
<u>Brenda Martin Linton</u>

<u>The Hem of His Garment: A Long Distance Prayer</u>

Lord, here I am standing...1200 miles away
Across the country...from where my sister Cora stay.
****

Right now she's sick...and not in the best of health
So Lord I'm pleading...but not for earthly wealth.
****

I'm pleading Lord...that you hear your servant's voice
I'm begging that Cora's life here...is also your choice.
****

I'm touching the hem of your garment...though Cora's far away...
I know that you can heal her here...on this earth today.
****

Lord let her stay here with us...a little while longer
Yes, heal her body and make my sister...healthy and stronger
****

I know that all power is in the hem of your precious robe...
So Jesus please...Honor my prayer...and the Bonds's Hope.
****

Jesus, We love her dearly...Yet we know you love her too
And Lord we are all doing all...that we know how to do!!!
****

I realize Lord that healing can come...only from the Hem
Of your Precious Cloak...
Just as the woman did back when...You were walking among a group of folk.
****

The woman had an issue of blood...for a very long, long time...
She inched and inched her way up to...the front of the line.

****

**She didn't mean to pass up others...And she didn't desire any recognition
All she knew was if she touched your cloak...She would have a blood transfusion.**

****

**So touching the hem of your garment...is Truly my Heart's prayer...
It's the only thing that I know for Cora...that could possibly save her**

****

**So Lord just hear us & honor...Our Prayer one more time...
Please forgive us Lord If we seem to pass up
others in the line!!!!!**

**Love,
Brenda (Cora's Baby sister)**

Jesus...Your reply to: A Long Distance Prayer

Well Lord, I still know that prayer...Is in the hem of your Robe
Even Though Saturday, January 5th...2002...My sweet sister took a Stroll.
****

She took a stroll from this earthly life...Into Life eternity...
Indeed she will be missed by us all...And that includes me.
****

Yes, Lord the prayer for our dear Cora...Was indeed to make Her Whole
We knew that it could be done...If she touched the hem of your robe.
****

We all had plans for Cora to be...Made whole here...on earth.
But your plan was quite different from ours...For You gave her soul a new Birth...

****

**A new birth...into eternity...Where she's in no more pain
Your Robe...Your Blood has washed her clean...Yes Health and strength she has regained.**

****

**Lord, yes we miss our sweet darling Cora...She will Always live in our Hearts
But Lord, the Bonds' Also know...One day we won't be apart.**

****

**We know that on Saturday, You looked from heaven above...And you said..."No More...My sweet child;
No more pain or Suffering and Because Of My Love...You'll Come to Heaven and Live in style."**

****

**You said "I know that on earth...you have many loved ones
You're a mother, Great Grandma, Grandma
Aunt...sister and wife...**

**But Come up here to heaven to live
with me...
I'm giving you eternal life**
****

**So now we know sweet Cora...is in
the best of care
For since she had to leave us...We
know she's Happy there;**

**Happy with and serving you Yes, We
know You love her too,
And Your sweet love surpasses
ours...so now
she's in heaven with you!!!**
****

*Take care of Cora, Jesus
See you in heaven, Cora*

*Love, From all of us
Including Me...Brenda (your baby sister)*

Brenda J. Martin-Linton

<u>Dedication to My Sister: Tall Rosa</u>

***To my sister Tall Rose*...#1...The third girl
of Ella Mae;**
In this ded-i-ca-tion to you...I have something
to say.

I have something **Rose** to say to you...About
our childhood years—
When I think about them now...It brings my
eyes to tears.

We didn't really get to know each other—We
went in separated directions—
So there're not many childhood memories...Of
sis-ter-ly affection.

But that's all right because we were...Still
reared in one family—
And that right there...especially means...a
great deal to me!!!

Mom gave us all the love she could...And kept us all together—
She provides us with food and clothing...And protection from the stormy weather.

But life sometimes does not allow...Peoples' lives to bind—
So these childhood years together...Memories are hard to find!!!

However, God has a way of mending...Things that seem to be broke
He has given us another chance as sisters...So where there's life there's hope.

The hope is now at our fingertips...We live only 16 miles apart—
We're closer now in our golden years...In our spirits and in our hearts!!!

<u>**It's funny that it took a move...Of 1200 miles from our birth home—**</u>
<u>**To get us back together...Wow!!! we're as close as our telephone.**</u>

I moved down here in '96…You joined me 8
months ago—
I'm so glad that you are here…I just want you
to know!!!

We've done so many sister things
together…Since your move down here.
That it makes up for the 50 year lost…Of all
our former years.

We have found out that…though our
lives…Have a 50 year spread—
We have so many things in common…From
our souls to our heads.

We cherish many of the same things…Such as
fashions and emotions—
We laugh at some of the similar jokes…And
have similar intuitions.

***We even trust God in a way that is…Dear to
our heart and soul—***
***We know that His love for us…Has redeemed
and made us whole!!!***

So Rose as I close this poem right now…And
end this dedication to you—*I thank God for
our reunion*…Here on earth and in heaven
too!!!

For I already know that our sisterly love…Will
be united with **God above**—
We will indeed share our eternity…***In the
presence of God's Love!!!***
Love,

***Your Sister in Christ as well as by Blood
Brenda Martin-Linton***

A Gift of Another Kind: Rap Christmas 2001

When you left the hospital and I came over
Your were trembling all the way up to your shoulders
It was then that I decided up in my mind
"Hey, my sister needs a gift of another kind"

Another kind meaning more than perfume or clothes
Neither did she need things for her bath or stove.
She needed a gift that's all for herself
So while shopping I took this blanket off the shelf!!!

It was really unique in that its temperature
controlled
It will keep you warm sis…eliminating the
cold
So when you get chilled…just whip it off
your shelf
Remember - Brenda bought it and say:
"<u>All for myself</u>"

I remember you wanted some slippers
too,
That you could easily slip your feet into…
So sister remember these gifts for
Christmas because
**They came from your sister Brenda,
not Santa Claus!**

Love,
Brenda

<u>Dedication to My Sister Rose #2</u>

***<u>Hello Rose number two—this
dedication's for you</u>***…The fourth of **Ella
Mae's** girls
Even though in miles we are distance
apart…To me you mean the world.

Yes, you mean the world to me Rosa #2.
'Cause sisters share such love
Love, that only **God** can give from **His
home**…From **Heaven above.**

I realize throughout these fifty long
years…Our lives have not been as close
As sisters should be throughout the
years…When bonding happens the most!

But that doesn't matter—**<u>Rose</u>**—
because…Sis-ter-ly love never ends
Neither fifty years—nor 1200
miles…Could hinder the joy I feel
when…

When we communicate by
telephone...Every moment we share
Oh how I cherish those wonderful
moments...The distance I can hardly
bear!

Those—wonderful times we spend
talking about...The **'happenings'** in our
lives
Bring such joy-to-my heart and
soul...And even tears—to my eyes!!!

I thank God for **you** Rose
especially...'Cause I feel the pain you've
had in life
But whether you realize it or not...***God
loved you through all of your strife.***

He loves you so much 'cause you're His
child...He has never left you alone.
What He wants from you MOST in this
life, Rose Is for Heaven to be your
home!!!

And this is not hard—He invited you in…When He stated, **"Come as you are!!!"**
Just accept my Lord Jesus at His Word…'Cause my **Lord** is never far!!!

Neither far from you and the one's that you love…Nor far from the one's that love you
But believe me, ***His Word***, you can count on…'Cause He told me- the same thing too!!!

So, as I end this dedication, **Rose #2**…I pray that you understand
That I thank God that our reunion in heaven—will be felt throughout the land.

For I know that our sisterly bond will be…
United in Heaven above
When we share our Life and Eternity…In the presence of God's love.

Love Always,
Your baby sister
Brenda Martin-Linton

March, 2002
<u>Happy Birthday Zeala, (My Niece)</u>

God bless you…and Happy Birthday
Zeala, You have such a gift,
For those in need…without
hesitation…You offer such a lift.

A lift in spirit…with such love…And so
much gentle care
You Zeala…give of your precious
time…You know just how to share.

I say, that because even though you were
ill…You gave much care and love,
To dear Poppy and to my loving sister
Cora…Who are both in heaven
above!!!!!!!

They both want…you to know…That
they are well pleased, Zeala…with you
And they wish you a Happy…Happy
Birthday…
And Zeala I do too!!!

With much love and many, many kisses,
Big Brenda (Cora and Poppy…At home
with Mom and the Lord.)
(Sorry, this Birthday card and gift was
late, but it was still in my heart on
your Birthday)

Dedication to my Niece: Corlisa Lyke Davis (Poppy)

The Storm is Over: My soul is free

Dear Momma...All my children...my dear friends and family—
My storm of life is over...So please don't cry for me.
All the suffering and the pain I had...Exist no more for me...
Though my body may be all you see...My soul has been set free!

Don't get me wrong—I am glad...We were placed in each others lives:
When God put us in the Bonds' family...We know that He was wise.
Because we loved each other...and didn't mind taking the slack...
When one of us...the Bonds' fell down...The others had their back!

'Cause God blessed me with 6 children: 4
daughters and 2 sons...
And as I got up in my years...He sent me
other ones;
Other related children to give a mothers
love...that they really lacked...
But as I said when one fell down—We all
had their back!!!

Now I am gone...I've done my best...So
please let me go—
I did all I could here on earth...Much love I
did show!!!
I'm happier now than ever before because
I've seen my Masters face—
He has taken Home to live with Him...By
His Mercy and His Grace.

You see the pain that I was in...was more
than I could bear:
The pain of cancer is excruciating...Pain I
would never want to share.
In God's own Mercy and Grace that
day...He embraced me in His arms
And He whispered "Dear Poppy" come with
me...You will be in no more harm.

Brenda J. Martin-Linton

So now the storm is over "you all"…My soul
has been set free…
And now for the very first time…I can
really, really see!
I can see God working at His Best…Cause
I'm in my Heavenly Home…
Now my soul is really free…And I will never
be alone!!!

Love to all of you…Poppy.

Written by Brenda J. Martin Linton

<u>Dedication to Ida:</u>
<u>An Eliminator of Strife</u>
SUB-TITLE: A TRUE FRIEND…*who*
determines to hear more than I say)
This Is Indeed A True Friend

Memories of how Brenda used to be…
Shows me—shunning people from my life;
I didn't want anyone in my life affairs…
My reason…***THIS WOULD***
ELIMINATE STRIFE!

After all, this was always…my way of thinking
I just wanted to be left alone;
But God, one day…sent me to Grace:
He appointed Grace as my Spiritual home.

I immediately obeyed—However I was
determined to remain,
True to the "single-handedness" of my affairs;
But God equipped one sister with spiritual
boldness—
To tackle that…her name: Ida Washington
Buress.

169

Her God-like approach was smooth: I can
remember saying;
"Ida Washington has something up her sleeve,"
But this "Spiritual Sister" was determined to
demonstrate.
God's mission...She was going to achieve.

Oh, she wasn't so bold- that she didn't...
Attempt God's mission- while allowing me my
space;
She just used the spirit of God's love an
compassion...
That Pastor Patten taught her at Grace.

You see- I hadn't realized this one thing,
God could perform His work through people;
So Ida's spiritual strength was very tough to
fight—
And rebellious trouble I gave her "A HEAP
OF"!!!

Oh, I fought hard to keep up my facade.
Determining- "Brenda you don't need a
friend;"
For I'd been alone—and I was going to
Keep that "solo" record till the bitter end.

I remember Ida calling—*to share the love of Christ*
With me over many times the telephone;
But I also remember saying in my
subconscious mind—
"Why doesn't she just leave me alone?"

After all, I had joined Grace—I had obeyed
God,
I thought to myself..."Isn't that enough??!!!
Because life had taught me this one lesson:
"Brenda you must remain independent and
tough.

Well, my "spiritual sister"—Ida Buress
With the Love of Christ in her heart;
Was used by God to tear down this wall
And has played in my life—*A GREAT*
PART!!!

She has proven to be...True to God's Word
Ida has indeed demonstrated a true friendship.
With this woman, who makes God her very life
style
We have formed a Christian kinship.

She has proven to be more than a friend-
She's walked by my side when I felt alone;
She has shared her love of Christ with me
With prayer...Encouragement...And thru
songs.

When I attempt to hide my problems from her
She's learned to listen not only to what I say...
Yes, Ida listens beyond...With her third ear
Very attentively...To what I don't state!!!

***This loving concern is part of her Christian
make up—***
She listens to my very hearts con-ver-sa-tion;
Now how she does this-Only God in Heaven
knows...
This has developed into an everlasting relation.

When I have been sick...She's came to my
aide—
Stating, "Brenda I'll do all that I can;"
Oh I thank God constantly God...For using her
As His missionary—"This spiritual woman."

When my husband died- She came one again
To do the things- I just couldn't bring myself
to do;
She practiced during that time—When a love
one dies...
A Christian friend during those
times...Remains true!!!

She's also been there at times...When I
couldn't attend—
The affairs for my daughters...April and Isis;
If she could help—she was right there.
Yes, Ida is definitely God—sent.

Oh, I could go o n...Trying to express—
God's Christian mission—Placing Ida in my
life;
But I will stop here and acknowledge His
Infinite Wisdom
Making me realize—*TRUE FRIENDSHIP*
ELIMINATES STRIFE!!!

God bless you and keep you
I love you Ida...Your Sister in Christ

Brenda J. Linton

<u>Dedication to My Christian Niece:</u>
<u>Nyree</u>
(Written January, 1995)

A Christian young lady befriended, April and
Isis…She later became my God-niece.
She possessed such a lovely innocent
spirit…***Her name was none other than
Nyree!!!***

When she first befriended my daughters at
church—I thought "she seems like a true
friend";
And over the years I have no regrets…For to
April and Isis—**Nyree is a God - send!!!**

Nyree is quite shy - **yet always a lady**…She
carries herself as a Christian should:
She presents herself in a Christ-like
manner…She only speaks as a Christian
would!!!

There are times Nyree tend to loose self-
confidence…In affairs I know she can
complete:

Yet, after a period of time—My niece
Nyree...Springs back displaying pride and
defeat!!!

My niece, Nyree displays so many artistic
talents...She amazes me with her many
creations:
Lord I'm so glad You sent Nyree into my
family...It's a blessing having her as a
relation!!!

A relation to us through, **Our Lord, Jesus
Christ**...I can think of no better 'tie',
When you are related through **My Lord and
Savior**...That bond lasts even after one dies!!!

I feel quite honored when she calls me **"Aunt
Brenda"**...This title aunt had to be earned"
We respect one another—and she knows I
care...Even times with her when I must be
firm!!!

I treasure the times when we go out to
eat...And the times when we just visit and talk:
It's nice having her come and visit...Her
conversation displays a Christian young lady's
walk!!!

I repeat Nyree "*I'M ESTHETIC*" you befriended April & Isis…You're a great God-niece to me,
You're indeed a God-sent blessing in the Linton's lives…And I'm glad **YOU ARE NYREE!!!**

May The Lord Richly Bless You,
Love Always
Your Aunt,

Brenda Martin-Linton

<u>Let's Rejoice With Doris: She is With our Lord!!!!!!!</u>
<u>(Written 10/31/94)</u>

Let's Rejoice with Doris—She's with Our Lord…She's very happy—That is no doubt;
Doris lived for this moment thru testimonies & songs…She's lived it day in & day out!!!

Doris lived a Christian Life—We all know that…Her walk was always for Christ;
She had a warm smile-showing her love for God…Yes, Doris, lived a true Christian life!!!

Whenever she spoke—she talked about God…She was proud when she spoke about Christ;
We all should follow her wonderful example…Speaking of Jesus in our everyday life!!!

She spoke of how good God was to her…We should rejoice because now He's even better;
For she's now with ***<u>The Word/ Truth/& The Light</u>***…Yet we must go on reading God's letter!

She had strong convictions speaking of
God…Yet, was gentle while speaking of his
Love;
The kind of reverence Sister Brooks
showed…Could come only from Our Lord
above!!

I remember one Christian song- that she
sang…<u>Oh, it is Jesus -It's- Jesus -in- my soul;</u>
<u>For I have touched the hem of His</u>
<u>Garment…**And His Blood has made me**</u>
<u>whole!!!</u>

These lyrics are more than mere words she
sang…For she really did have Jesus in her
soul;
Tho' we say she has died, **<u>'She's Just</u>**
<u>Touched His Garment"</u>…
Now, indeed, **<u>She Has Been Made Whole!!!</u>**

Doris has just taken her eternal stroll with
Jesus…A transition we call ***"from life to***
death'*;*

But the reverse is true-for now she's
alive...**She has Eternal Life & Everlasting
Health!!**

So **<u>Rejoice</u>** I say, **<u>Rejoice</u>** in My Lord...For
His mercy rocked Doris to sleep;
He lovingly said "You've suffered
enough"..."Now your soul I will bring back to
me."

"Doris you'll be missed by all: you were easy
to love...A Christian: Wife, Mother & Friend;
Though your presence with us is now
terminated...Your life's story will never end!!!

So let's remember her singing *<u>'Oh It Is
Jesus'</u>*...Let's remember the Christian life she
lived;
*Let's <u>Rejoice</u> and celebrate her new
destination...**For she has given us all she can
give!!!***

So to her Christian & immediate family-I

offer these words... I pray they bring some
comfort to your soul;
For we all share in the loss of 'Our Sister
Brooks'...But let's **"REJOICE NOW"**—For
Now She's Been Made Whole!!!

DORIS IS WITH OUR LORD!!!

Written by Sister Brenda J. Martin-Linton
In Memory of Sister Doris Condolences from
Grace Baptist Church Choir

<u>Dedication to Oma Hughes- My Christian Sister</u>

God led me to Grace Baptist Church…He said "Brenda there you'll be fed!"
I obeyed and gave my service to Grace…There by Pastor Patten, I have been led.

During my service at this church…
God's blessed me to meet some dear friends;
One is a teacher name Oma Hughes…She's been with me through thick and thin!!!

I had some trials during our Christian tie…I've had some great needs in my life;
She's one sister who's readily come to my aid…Her presence always reflected my Christ.

Like the times when I…had to leave town: Just to inform her, I had no regrets;
Because Oma would agree to take care of my house…Stating," Brenda I'd be glad to do that."

When I had been sick on several occasions...She would prepare some food for me to eat;
She would even go grocery shopping for me...When I couldn't get up on my feet!

When my daughter, Isis, was in her classroom...Oma Hughes taught her very well;
For the knowledge she instilled in my daughter, Isis...Is more than I can tell!!!

Oh, to see her on might think "**Oh, she is small**"...Just let me leave this thought with you;
Oma may be small in stature but...She does what she has to do!!!

If one couldn't see the height of this lady...But just knew she had a hard task;
They'd see she could run rings around the problem...Tackling it to the very last!

She's shown me in our Christian walk together...That she is indeed a Child of Christ;
I thank the Lord with all of my soul...That He brought Oma into my life.

There's been times I need a friend to
listen…To things I felt in my soul;
With an attentive ear, Oma was there…Her
concern being warm—**NOT COLD!**

I pray that my Christian friendship to
*Oma…*Is as meaningful to her regarding me;
I could never repay her for what she has
done…To assist me in my times of need.

As I end this dedication in regards to Oma…I
treasure our Christian Love;
'Cause we both know that this Christian
Sisterhood…Came from Jesus, Our Lord
above.

Your Sister in Christ,

Brenda Martin Linton

<u>To Ethel: My Christian Sister</u>

Hello Ethel, this dedication I write to you…You're indeed a loving friend
I pray this bond that we share…Shall never—ever—end!!!

You see you are a true Christian sister…I hold you dear to my heart
You have taken a special place in my life…One that shall never part.

Never part because—you're always there…As a friend I can turn to
We've talked—we've shared—we've cried together…Our friendship remains ever true.

You've understood—when I've had problems…You've joined me in prayer and song

You've given assistance whenever I
needed...And sheltered me in your
blessed home.

When I visited Chicago, you open your
door...No matter the day or the hour
Only God gives this love—to Christian
friends...**Only God can give this
power.**

*I pray that I return this Christian
love*...To you as you have shown to me
'Cause you deserve friendship as well as
giving it...I pray that I have shown it to
thee.

*Your Christian walk is one of
love*...I've seen how you display Jesus
Christ
I know without a doubt, when this life is
over...That you'll inherit eternal life.

Eternal Life, what a "Hallelujah Blessing"...One could ask for nothing more
Jesus will welcome you Ethel with open arms...When you reach that magnificent shore.

So, I pray that when we both meet Jesus, *He'll say...* "**This—friendship—truly indeed—**
This friendship that you both shared on earth...Will be magnified up here with me."

So, as this dedication end I want you to know...In your—soul—mind and heart
That a friendship like this could only be made in heaven...Where true friendships get their start!!!

Love,
Your Christian sister,

Brenda Martin-Linton

To Cookie: A Dear Friend

To Cookie—truly—a dear friend…For me
you've al-ways been there
When I really needed a friend…You were one
who really cared.

I know that our friendship started…@20
years ago with my girls
But since that time you have proven—You're
one of my best friends in the world.

Like I said this friendship started…Way back
in the past
But some how—it has managed…To last—and
last—and last.

I can remember the day that I entered…That
Day Camp with April and Isis
How you took up a genuine concern…Despite
of the "interrogation crisis!!!

Yes, I know…I bombarded you…With a
million of my concerns—
*Because—there were so many things…***That I**
had to learn!

Brenda J. Martin-Linton

I had to learn if this Day Camp…Was the best
place for their welfare
**I had to really know if my girls…<u>Were in
the best of care.</u>**

Well during their stay at this camp…You took
their safety and care—
As a #1 priority just as you did…For all the
campers there.

I remember the times when I was late…It
didn't phase you one way or the other—
You'd just take them by their hands…And take
them with you to your mother.

***Both of you made sure they ate…They were
indeed in the best of care***
'Cause when I'd arrive to pick them up…They
were full, safe and happy there.

You can't imagine how I appreciated…Your
'Auntly' and **'genuine'** provisions—
I'm truly so glad I chose that camp…**It was
indeed a wise decision.**

And since that time 20+ years ago...You've
also shown Christian love
To our family—which I know...Was "love"
sent from above.

For when I've shared personal
problems...Whether I ranted, cried or raved—
**Our Christian bond was never broken...No
matter how I may have behaved.**

I know sometimes we didn't agree...or see eye
to eye on things—
But I can't remember even one time...Where
this stopped us from speaking!!

Your Christian love for the girls and I...Has
surely passed all the test
I can say—of all my friends...You are truly
one of the best!

**So again I repeat this to you, Cookie...This
dedication from my heart—
Our friendship was indeed made in
Heaven...And in that we shall never part.**

Because when my Lord—Jesus binds…People
on earth in Christian love
*That Christian Friendship will last and
last…Eternally up above!!!*

So as I close—in paper and pen…This
Cookie—I want to say—
**Thank God our true Christian Love…Will
extend beyond Judgment Day!!!!!**

Christian Love Always,

On Earth and in Heaven—

Your Christian Sister,

Brenda Martin -Linton

A Dedication: To Alfay White

*To Al - fay my friend…*Though we met not
long ago—
Your Christian friendship has indeed—proven
true…
We met at work—just about…One and a half
years ago
Yet at this time—**"I take my hat—Off to
you."**

I say this with all respect…You are a great
friend indeed—
During this time we have both learned to
share…
Our—problems—Our concerns—Our great
Christian Love;
Yes, thru Christ we have learned how to care.

It amazes me—how—on oc-ca-sion—that
we—don't tend to mind
A 3:00—a.m.—call on the phone—
If there's a problem—we can't sleep…and are
worried deep inside…
We don't mind if our phone rings at home.

You have listened—you've advised…You have lend-ed an ear
You have even given me—wise and friendly advice
Even though you've been a friend for just over a year…
Alfay…Christian friendship—indeed—is so nice!!!

There's one thing really appealing to me—
About you Alfay,
Is your belief—And love for Our Christ—
That's why I know that you are…Indeed a
Chris-tian friend
And in Heaven we will share—**Eternal Life.**

So as this pen begin to stop…**To End**—this
dedication—
I know that this—Friendship is—from above…
I also know that this Christian love…That we
share here on earth
Will continue…thru **Eternal Life**—up above.

A Christian Friend Always,

Brenda Martin-Linton

<u>Dedication To Jean: A Christian Sister</u>

Jean, Jean a friend indeed…Sometimes we
talk and share—
Our Christian views and Love for Christ—And
the burdens that we bear.

Burdens that we as humans…Have down here
on earth below—
Nevertheless, our Christian love…We always
try to show.

*Even though Jean, in our Christian
walk…Spans of silence have been there—*
But when we do talk on the telephone…We
express how much we care…

Care about each others walk down here…With
Jesus Christ as our Savior…
We really try to exemplify…The true Chris -
tian behavior.

And even though we do not always
see…Things eye to eye…
*One thing we agree on most of all…Is
Walking the Christian Life.*

**And that to me is of utmost
importance**…Jean, in our Christian Walk
'Cause that in itself gives us enough
conversation…To talk…and talk—and talk.'

For I realize—in every Christian walk…Each
one allows you to grow—
In different ways for the will of the Lord…So
that you will know…

That all of God's Children show different
aspects…Of the many faces of Our Christ
**That's why I am so happy Jean…We share
this Christian Life!!!**

For I know that when we get to Heaven…And
meet our Father Above—
**He'll say, "Jean and Brenda I am so proud
that…You were sisters in Christian Love."**

So as this dedi-cation ends…I want you to
know this…**Jean**
**That having you as a Christian
sister……Has been rather keen!!!**

With Love,
Your Sister in Christ,
Brenda Martin-Linton

<u>Valentine's Day Poetry: (1994)</u>

<u>*HAPPY VALENTINE'S DAY TO APRIL AND ISIS*</u>

To my two
daughters…April and
Isis—
My two daughters,
whom I truly adore;
If the Lord had blessed
me with ten more
hearts
I couldn't love you
more!

So in this 19-94 "Love
Time Season—
There're two things I
want to say:
"I love you both, with
all of my heart…
And Happy '95
Valentine's Day!!!

VALENTINE EXPRESSIONS TO MY Husband

(I wrote these 12 expressions of love for Leonard for Valentines Day February 14, 1994. My dearly beloved Leonard sadly and unexpectingly passed away February 23, 1994...two weeks after I wrote these poems for him.)

Please be 'My Valentine' dear—
I won't have it any other way;
Indeed, I am blessed...to be with you
On this 1994 Valentine's Day!!!
▪▪▪

Valentine's Day is my day to express
This deep love I have for you, honey;
For indeed you are "my angel sent from heaven...
I wouldn't trade you for all of "earth's money"!!!!!
▪▪▪

Valentine's Day should be everyday—
Especially with a mate like you;
A marriage like ours was made in heaven...
With God's seal of approval too!!!
▪▪▪

On this Valentine's Day…I want to say,
"Darling Leonard, I love you so much…that
Whenever you say, I love you Brenda…I get
weak
I feel faint from your sweet "vocal touch"!!!
■■■

It's so sweet being loved by you…Leonard,
It's great being your "Valentine"
I'm so glad we are together sharing our
love—
I'm so glad that I'm yours and you're
mine!!!
■■■

I am yours on this Glorious Valentine's
Day…
Leonard, my love for you is so dear;
I pray with all of my heart and soul
That your presence…is always near!!!
✻✻✻✻✻✻✻✻✻✻✻✻✻✻✻✻✻✻✻✻✻✻✻✻✻✻✻✻✻✻✻✻✻✻✻✻✻✻

It's so sweet being loved by you…
It's so nice being your Valentine;
I'm so glad we're together—sharing our
love…
I'm so glad that I'm yours and you're
mine!!!!!
■■■

**On this Valentine's Day—I would like to
express
This deep love I possess for you...
I also know the way you make me feel
You love me very deeply too!!!**

**This Valentine's Day of 1994
I crown you Leonard, as my best friend:
I'm so glad that we are "husband and
wife"...
I pray that "our love" never ends!!!**

**Happy Valentine's Day...My sweet
Darling—
I'm so glad that I love you:
I wouldn't find a truer love anywhere like
you, Leonard
If I searched the whole world through!!!**

**On this 1994 Valentine's Day
I'm glad you're the "love of my life"
I can't think of any better role to be in
Than we have...as husband and wife!!!**

Hip, Hip, Hooray!!! We're alive
Spending Valentine's Day together in '94...
I pray that that we spend the rest of our
lives
Expressing our great love...forevermore!!!
****

Leonard, I have so many expressions of love
that I don't know which one to give you. So
I present all of these poetic expressions of
love to you. I pray that we spend a "zillion"
more Valentine's Day together.

Love,
Your wife forever...Brenda Linton

December 11, 2000

Dear Mr. Goetz,
(Day 1)

It's Christmas time 2000...And your
Santa has some gifts,
To present to you...Before we "break"
this week.
However, its way too early to reveal
my identity,
But by Friday, my identity you'll not
seek!!!!

You see each day I'll reveal...More
about myself
So you can become more familiar with
your Secret Santa
But at this point there're two things
that you must know
Is that I like poetry......And I'm not
from Atlanta.

Ha, Ha, Ha!!!!!!!!!

Merry Christmas,
XXXXXXXXXXXXXXXXXXXXXXXXX

Your Secret Santa

December 12, 2000

Dear Mr. Goetz:

Well here I am again…dropping a
hint-
About your Secret Santa…For the
<u>second day</u> to you:
Well, here's something for you to
think about right now
I'm a teacher here…And I believe that
your concerns for Coop are true.

For I've presented several ideas to
you…
Since your arrival here…
Though I had inhibitions when you
first came;
But each time that I've stated my
situations to you…
My "inhibitions" have been calmed
and put to shame.

So I hope that this information...Puts
you closer Mr. Goetz
To recognizing your Secret Santa this
year;
You'll hear more about my
identity...As this workweek closes...
So Merry Christmas...And Hap—py
New Year!!!

Your Secret Santa,

XXXXXXXXXXXXXXXXXXXXXXXX

December 13, 2000

Dear Mr. Goetz,

**Well, here I am for the *third day*...Your—Secret Santa
Trying to leave you a hint...And a clue;
A clue about who I am...Yes, my identity
So Mr. Goetz...*This is what I'll do!!!!!***

**I will tell you this about myself...I love Free Expression
In fact I love "The Arts"...Just as you do too;
But we all express ourselves in very different ways...
I have even expressed *my joy of art* to you!!!**

I also have an appreciation…For
working with my students
In all areas that may enrich their
young lives;
Yes, poetically I've tried to show
you…My identity, Mr. Goetz
But if you can't guess… *You must
wait—till day five!!!*

So as I close this short poetic…Secret
Santa note—
I'll repeat this well known
closing…For you;
*Merry Christmas, Happy New Year, and
God's many blessings…*
*I extend this to your family…And to
you.*

Your Secret Santa,
XXXXXXXXXXXXXXXXXXXXXXXXX

December 14, 2000

Dear Mr. Goetz,

**Your Secret Santa's here again…The
4th day with a hint Mr. Goetz.
About my true i-den-ti-ty…
But just in case you have no clue as to
who I am yet…
I will give another hint concerning me.**

**Just combine all the small
clues…Together, Mr. Goetz…
You know I write, I love the
Arts…And I teach;
One more clue for you is that I express
myself with words
In another way than through verbal
speech!!!**

**Well I real-ly do believe…"That" clue
rings a bell
For you to recognize…My true i-den-
ti-ty…**

But just in case you're still not sure of who I really am
You've only 1 day left to guess…About me.

So until tomorrow I will close this Secret Santa note…
With some words to bring much joy and much cheer;
To your family…To your loved ones and all that you know
Mr. Goetz: *Merry Christmas…Happy New Year!!!!*

Your Secret Santa,

XXXXXXXXXXXXXXXXXXXXXXXX

December 15, 2000

Dear Mr. Goetz,

Yes, this *fifth day* has finally arrived...For your Secret Santa
To leave a hint about <u>her</u> i-den-ti-ty;
I do believe that this...Tiny hint above
With the other clues lead you *straight to me!!!*

Well now—you should know...What I really like to do
For you have seen me perform on many occasions...
With my students in ways to help enrich their lives
To help them grow in all forms of their education.

***Oops!!!* I know I really gave away my identity**
Because all these clues leaves you straight to my name;
I'm glad I had the chance this year to be your Secret Santa
In fact we're all happy that it's Coop where you came.

And I hope that you liked your *Secret Santa's* gifts
Which you've received all this week here at School;
I really believe that you guessed my identity from the start
But you just decided…*"To keep your cool"!*

So as I end this poetic Secret Santa's note
Let me make this last statement quite clear…
I pray that your family has these two things:
A Merry Christmas and a Happy New Year!!!!!

Now your *Former* Secret Santa of 2000
Mrs. XXXXXX-XXXXXX

The Beginning and the End: Until We Meet Again

One might wonder how **Life Line Productions** *began*...and how this Company...***will end***. Well, let me begin by saying that the **alpha** and **omega** stage was and is orchestrated by Our Lord and Savior, Jesus Christ. **Life Line Productions** was initiated truly well before my birth. I believe that God chose me to write well before I knew that I was writing...and why I was writing. It was as though He planted a seed inside of me before I even was formed in my mother's womb. God had His own reason for allowing this seed to spring up in me. For whatever reason He did, I am excited **that He did**. As far as my awareness of **"Our Close Relationship"** through writing one day, it started 30+ years ago. I just started writing. I never even thought of doing anything with these writings. All I know is that I had to give "flesh" to what I felt were ***expressions from my heart*** in regards to my **Life Line** to Jesus...***My Walk With the Lord***. These expressions were my **Life Line** to God and with God. Sometimes I could just be walking...riding along in my car…or just meditating!!! These expressions would begin to burn a yearning in my soul to be "penned". So I would write them down…I would write them down **at that time.** Situations, yearnings and longings in my soul just begged to be expressed for the Lord and for His presence in my Life. **So again, I would write.** There were many, many times I would be awakened from my sleep by the Lord's presence…And I had to jump up in the stillness of the night and write the songs…these expressions…these burnings deep in my soul as to my experiences with the Lord…"I had to pen" how **He** was walking and talking with me. It got so that during certain periods of my life I even had to sleep with a pad and pencil besides my bed…I knew that if the **Lord** gently woke me up to write…that I had to be ready.

Now at this point in my life, a *half century in age,* the Lord has inspired me to share these expressions with you. So being obedient to my Lord and Savior, I am *'penning'* theses poems of inspiration, dedications and expressions. I pray that they serve as inspirations in your Life as well. I pray that somewhere inside the confines of this book, something touches your

spirit—your heart—and your situation.
Yes, the names expressed in this book may be
different…those who touched my life may be
different from your loved ones; however, I
pray that the "heart" of the inspirations can
mean as much to you as it did to me at the time
of that particular phase in my life…I pray that
something written in this book may align up
with something in your life…***Your
existence…*Your Life Line with The Lord.**
I don't know how **Life Line** will end or come
to a close; prayerfully it won't take me another
30- 50 years to share what may show as an
inspiration to you in your **Life. During these
30+ years many of my loved ones have gone
on to be with the Lord, including my
beloved mother, Ella Mae Bonds and my
darling husband, Mr. Marion Leonard
Linton. My two wonderful daughters have
now graduated from college and now one
has given her life in a full time ministry and
the other one is exemplifying God in her life
everyday. I can indeed say that God has
been a Life Line Productions even thru my
children. It greatly saddened me when my
baby girl, Isis, left, but she stated that the
Lord had called her to another more distant
location to a ministry. At this time, I'm**

asking the Lord to watch over her and to quiet my heart about the distance. On the day of her departure she left a poem which I found after she had left; it went like this...

My Wings

Tonight I told you what I believe to be
God's undeniable plan for me...
You were upset...And I wondered why!!!

Could it be that you are losing your baby?
Maybe...
Could it be you'll be in an empty home
alone?
Or maybe that you'll miss me...Gee!

In a way I assumed you would be somewhat
happy.
I am after all your most "Expensive Child".
The one you thought would always run wild,
Remember?

I was the one who could eat for eight...
When I was trying to watch my weight...

I would eat 2 chicken breasts for dinner
And used to get sick in the winter!

Other moms would not care about my
spectacle thickness...
and how this would render me friendless.
<u>But not you momma...You have always
tried to do what's best for me,</u>
With no regard to your well being, health or
safety...
So, I thank you "mom" for many a
sacrifice...
And instilling in me a love for Christ...Our
Lord
And although you were upset tonight about
me, Isis, your baby
I promise not to cut and only snip away at
the cord.

Because truth be told,
Had you not ranted, raved and cried,
I would have deemed all the aforementioned
as lies.
So mama, thanks for wanting me to stay,
While continuing to build the muscles in my
wings...

215

**In Him and forever,
Your Baby,
Isis**

Yes, though I do confess that though my heart is saddened because of her distant departure, I do rejoice that God has been a <u>Life Line</u> even thru my seed. It is indeed my daily prayer that I will be blessed even more so by the Lord to have more time to spend on writing and sharing with others *His Love* not only for me, but for anyone and everyone who is touched by having their own personal **Life Line.** However, if we never meet again here on this earth through **Life Line Productions**., be assured that we shall **all** meet in Heaven where **we will experience** that <u>**Eternal Life Line with Jesus/ The Father and our dear loved ones.**</u>

Till We Meet Again,

Life Line Productions or
Lifeline with Jesus [Creator]

Brenda Martin-Linton
[Author]

Brenda J. Martin-Linton

<u>From the Author's Desk:</u>

To sum up my life…well, I started off as a seed planted by the Lord. After being blessed to be "born", my life span has encountered many roles such as daughter, educator, friend, wife, mother, widower, writer and all the other roles one assumes just being in this world. However, the one role that has consumed my entire existence is that of being a child of God. As you read these inspirations…these dedications…these songs…I challenge you to take a journey with me as a child of God as I share with you "<u>My Walk With The Lord.</u>"

Author

Brenda J. Martin-Linton
Life Line Productions

Printed in the United States
17046LVS00001B/166-180